ON THE CHRONICLES OF CEYLON

ON THE CHRONICLES OF CEYLON

BY

BIMALA CHURN LAW

GYAN

Published by

GYAN

Gyan Publishing House
5, Ansari Road
Daryaganj, New Delhi-110002
Phone: 011-47034999, 9811692060
E-mail: books@gyanbooks.com

Distribution Network
gyanbooks.com
India, USA, Canada, UK, Australia, France

ISBN : 978-81-212-3847-2 (PB)
First Published, 1947

2nd Impression 2020

Printed at: Gyan Press, Delhi.

The book at your disposal is the edition of an old book originally published long back. The Text quality of this book may not be at par as compared to our other books but many readers approached us to reprint this important book so that it could satiate their hunger. We request all the readers of this book to help us to improve its quality by providing the necessary text of those pages which are not properly visible. Your valuable support in this case will be highly appreciated and acknowledged and our future readers will be benefitted immensely.

THE CHRONICLES OF CEYLON

By BIMALA CHURN LAW

D.Litt., Ph.D., M.A., B.L.

President, Calcutta Geographical Society, Iran Society, Prācyavāṇī Mandira, Indian Research Institute, Royal Asiatic Society of Bengal; Honorary Fellow, Royal Asiatic Society of Great Britain and Ireland; Fellow, Royal Asiatic Society (Bombay Branch); Fellow, Royal Asiatic Society of Bengal; Hony. Correspondent to the Archaeological Survey of India; Hony. Member, Bhandarkar Oriental Research Institute and Gaṅganath Jha Research Institute; Corporate Member, American Oriental Society; Fellow, Royal Geographical Society of London; Author, *Aśvaghoṣa, Buddhaghosa, History of Pali Literature, Tribes in Ancient India, Geography of Early Buddhism, Geographical Essays, India as described in early texts of Buddhism and Jainism, Concepts of Buddhism, Mahāvīra : His Life and Teachings, etc., etc.*

PUBLISHED BY THE ROYAL ASIATIC SOCIETY OF BENGAL,
1 PARK STREET, CALCUTTA

PREFACE

In this treatise an attempt has been made to present a careful and exhaustive study of the chronicles of Ceylon in a spirit of scientific research. In 1908 Geiger made a critical study of this subject for the first time in his work on *The Dīpavaṃsa and Mahāvaṃsa and their Historical development of Ceylon.* In 1928 G. P. Malalasekera published a book on the *Pali Literature of Ceylon* (*J.R.A.S.* publication, Prize Publication Fund, Vol. X) and in 1933 I, in my *History of Pali Literature,* dealt with the same topic. In the present book my treatment is different from that of the previous writers. In three chapters I have discussed the chronological, literary, and historical position of the chronicles in Pali and Sinhalese. I have tried to utilize all the available materials, which may be gathered from ancient and modern literature on the subject. This work is, I believe, new in its treatment, and will remove a long-felt want. I shall consider my labour amply rewarded, if it be of some use to scholars interested in the Ceylonese chronicles.

Calcutta,
43 Kailas Bose Street,
February, 1947.

BIMALA CHURN LAW.

CONTENTS

BIBLIOGRAPHY

1. Academy, September, 1874.
2. Ancient India as described by Megasthenes and Arrian (J. W. McCrindle, 1926).
3. Asoka (D. R. Bhandarkar, 2nd Ed., 1932).
4. Asoka (Radhakumud Mookerji, 1928).
5. Asoka and His Inscriptions (B. M. Barua, 1946).
6. Aśvaghoṣa (B. C. Law, R.A.S.B. Monograph Series, Vol. I, 1946).
7. Buddhadatta's Manual (A. P. Buddhadatta, 1915).
8. Buddhaghosa (B. C. Law, Bombay Branch Royal Asiatic Society, Monograph No. I, 1946).
9. Buddhavaṃsa (*J.P.T.S.*, 1882).
10. Buddhist India (T. W. Rhys Davids).
11. Buddhist Records of the Western World (S. Beal).
12. Buddhist Suttas (Rhys Davids, S.B.E., Vol. XI).
13. Cambodian Mahāvaṃsa (*J.R.A.S.*, 1902).
14. Catalogue Du Fonds, Tibetan (Cordier).
15. Catalogue of Sinhalese Manuscripts (Wickremasinghe).
16. Catalogue of the Chinese Translation of the Buddhist Tripiṭaka (Bunyiu Nanjio).
17. Ceylon Lectures (B. M. Barua).
18. Cūḷavaṃsa (Ed. Geiger, *P.T.S.*).
19. Dāṭhāvaṃsa (Ed. and Tr. B. C. Law, 1925).
20. Dāṭhāvaṃsa (Tr. M. Coomaraswamy, 1874).
21. Debates Commentary (Eng. Tr. of Kathāvatthuppakaraṇa-aṭṭhakathā by B. C. Law, *P.T.S.*).
22. Dhātumālā.
23. Dhātuvaṃsa.
24. Dictionary of Pali Proper Names, 2 Vols. (G. P. Malalasekera).
25. Dīpavaṃsa (Ed. and Tr. Oldenberg, 1879).
26. Dīpavaṃsa (Tr. E. M. Coomaraswamy, 1908).
27. Dīpavaṃsa and Mahāvaṃsa (Geiger).
28. Dīpavaṃsa und Mahāvaṃsa und die Geschichtliche überlieferung in Ceylon (Geiger, Leipzig, 1905).
29. Divyāvadāna (Cowell and Neil).
30. Early History of Buddhism in Ceylon (E. W. Adikaram).
31. Epigraphia Zeylanica, Vols. I and III.
32. Extended Mahāvaṃsa (Ed. G. P. Malalasekera, R.A.S. Ceylon Branch).
33. Gandhavaṃsa (*J.P.T.S.*, 1886).
34. History of Pali Literature, 2 Vols. (B. C. Law).
35. Holy Bible—St. Matthew.
36. India as described in early texts of Buddhism and Jainism (B. C. Law).
37. Indian Antiquary, Vol. XXXV.
38. Indian Culture, Vol. XII.
39. Indian Historical Quarterly, Vol. VIII.
40. *J.A.S.B.*, 1837.
41. *J.B.B.R.A.S.*, XI, 1875.
42. *J.P.T.S.*, 1886, 1902-3.
43. *J.R.A.S.*, 1896, 1898, 1902, 1905, 1906.
44. *J.R.A.S.*, Ceylon Branch, XXIII.
45. Jātaka (Fausböll).
46. Journal of the Department of Letters, Vol. I (Calcutta University).
47. Kathāvatthuppakaraṇa-aṭṭhakathā (*J.P.T.S.*, 1889).
48. Le Dāṭhāvança : On Histoire de la dent relique du Buddha Gotama, 1884.
49. Legend of the Topes (Eng. Tr. of Thūpavaṃsa by B. C. Law, *Bibliotheca Indica*, 1945).

50. Mahābhārata (Vaṅgavāsī Ed.).
51. Mahābodhivaṃsa (*P.T.S.*).
52. Mahāvaṃsa (Geiger's Ed. and Tr., *P.T.S.*).
53. Mahāvaṃsa (Turnour's Ed. and Tr., 1837).
54. Mahāvaṃsa (H. Sumangala and Baṭuwanṭudawe, Colombo, 1905).
55. Mahāvaṃsa (Eng. Tr. by L. C. Wijesinha, 1909).
56. Mahāvaṃsa (Sinhalese Tr. by Wijesinha, 1889).
57. Manorathapūraṇī (*P.T.S.*).
58. Manual of Buddhist Historical Traditions (Eng. Tr. of Saddhammasaṅgaha by B. C. Law, 1941).
59. Manual of Indian Buddhism (Kern).
60. Milindapañho (Ed. V. Trenckner).
61. Minor Anthologies of the Pali Canon, Pt. III—Buddhavaṃsa and Cariyā-piṭaka (Eng. Tr. by B. C. Law, S.B.B., Vol. IX, 1938).
62. Nalāṭadhātuvaṃsa.
63. Nikāya Saṅgrahawa (Tr. C. M. Fernando, 1908; edited by Gunawardhana).
64. On Yuan Chwang's travels in India by Thomas Watters (edited by T. W. Rhys Davids and S. W. Bushell, 1904).
65. Pali Literature of Ceylon (G. P. Malalasekera).
66. Paramatthadīpanī on Therīgāthā (*P.T.S.*).
67. Paṭisambhidāmagga (*P.T.S.*)
68. Petavatthu (*P.T.S.*)
69. Points of Controversy (*P.T.S.* Tr. Series).
70. Pūjāvalīya, Colombo Ed., 1897.
71. Rājāvalīya (Tr. by B. Guṇasekara, Colombo, 1900).
72. Rājaratnākaraya, Colombo, 1887; edited by Simon de Silva, Colombo, 1907.
73. Saddhammasaṅgaha (Ed. N. Saddhānanda, *J.P.T.S.*, 1890).
74. Samantapāsādikā (*P.T.S.*).
75. Sāratthappakāsinī (*P.T.S.*).
76. Sāsanavaṃsa (*P.T.S.*).
77. Some Kṣatriya Tribes of Ancient India (B. C. Law).
78. Study of the Mahāvastu and its Supplement (B. C. Law).
79. Sumaṅgalavilāsinī (*P.T.S.*).
80. Thūpavaṃsa (Ed. B. C. Law).
81. Thūpavaṃsa (Sinhalese Ed. Dhammaratana, 1896).
82. University of Ceylon Review, Vols. II and IV.
83. Uttaravihāra Mahāvaṃsa.
84. Vaṃsatthappakāsinī, 2 Vols. (*P.T.S.*).
85. Vimānavatthu (*P.T.S.*).
86. Vinaya Piṭaka (*P.T.S.*).
87. Vuttamālā (Upatapassī).
88. Wiener Zeitschrift für die Kunde des Morgenlandes, Vol. XXI.
89. Zeitschrift den Deutschen Morgenländischen Gesellschaft, 63, 1909.

Chapter I

CHRONOLOGICAL POSITION

It is not unreasonably claimed that so far as the Buddhist world is concerned, the Theras of Ceylon stand unrivalled in the field of Chronicles narrating not only the political history of their island but also the ecclesiastical history of their faith. If the *Dīpavaṃsa* is the oldest known Pali chronicle produced in Ceylon, the *Sāsanavaṃsadīpa* by Thera Vimalasāra is certainly the latest one (1929). In between the two we have first of all general introductions to the *Sumaṅgalavilāsinī* and a few other commentaries written by Buddhaghosa, the pioneer Pali commentator, and after that the general introduction to the *Samantapāsādikā*, the *Mahāvaṃsa* by Mahānāma in its two recensions, the *Mahābodhivaṃsa*, the *Dīpavaṃsaṭṭhakathā*, the *Vaṃsatthappakāsinī*, the *Dāṭhāvaṃsa*, the *Thūpavaṃsa*, the *Cetiyavaṃsaṭṭhakathā*, the *Nalāṭadhātuvaṃsa*, and the *Saddhammasaṅgaha*, all written in Pali, and, above all, the *Cūḷavaṃsa* representing the continuation of the *Mahāvaṃsa* through its later supplements. In the list one must include also such Sinhalese writings as the *Pūjāvalī*, the *Nikāyasaṅgraha*, the *Dhātuvaṃsa*, the *Rājāvalī*, the *Rājaratnākara* and *Vuttamālā*. Although we have a masterly dissertation on the chronological position of these works from the pen of Geiger, it is necessary to reconsider it before dealing with their literary position.

1. *Dīpavaṃsa*.[1]—The main reason advanced for regarding this Pali Chronicle of Ceylon as a work of antiquity is that it stands, as distinguished from the rest which are chronologically later, as the literary production of a school or community, and not as the composition of an individual author. It is considered to be the last of the literary works of Ceylon which had no special authors.[2] Oldenberg places the closing date of the *Dīpavaṃsa* in its extant form between the beginning

---

[1] *Vide* Oldenberg Ed. and Tr. (1879); Geiger Ed. and Tr. (*P.T.S.*, 1908 and 1912); Geiger, *Dīpavaṃsa und Mahāvaṃsa und die geschichtliche überlieferung in Ceylon*, Leipzig 1905; Tr. by E. M. Coomaraswamy, Colombo, 1908; *Z.D.M.G.*, 63, 1909, 540ff.; *Indian Antiquary*, XXXV, p. 443; *Wiener Zeitschrift für die Kunde des Morgenlandes*, Vol. XXI, pp. 203 and 307. The *Dīpavaṃsa* puts together some well-known traditions handed down among the Buddhists of Ceylon sometimes in a clumsy manner. For historical and geographical data from this chronicle (*Vide* B. C. Law, *History of Pali Literature*, II, Chap. VI, pp. 555ff.).

[2] Malalasekera, *The Pali Literature of Ceylon*, p. 132.

of the fourth and the first third of the fifth century A.D.[1] Malalasekera while discussing the question of its closing date significantly observes: 'It could not have been closed before the beginning of the fourth century, because its narrative extends till about A.D. 302. Buddhaghosa quotes several times from the *Dīpavaṃsa*, but his quotations differ in some details from our version. In the *Mahāvaṃsa* we are told that Dhātusena (459–77) ordered the *Dīpavaṃsa* to be recited in public at the annual Mahinda festival, so that by that time the *Dīpavaṃsa* had been completed. After that date it fell into disuse, its glory outdone by the more brilliant work of Mahānāma; but it seems to have been studied till much later, because Dhammakitti III of the Āraṇyakavāsī sect quotes it in his *Saddhammasaṅgaha* (p. 47, v. 7; p. 49, vv. 8 foll.) with great respect as a work of much merit and immense importance.'[2]

The important question which arises at the outset is—what was the exact form of this chronicle, when king Dhātusena caused it to be recited in public year after year during the Mahinda festival? To put it in other words, did the narrative of the *Dīpavaṃsa*, as it was then known, extend beyond the advent of Mahinda in the island and the establishment of the Good Faith through his efforts? Evidently it did not extend beyond this great event in the early history of Ceylon. It is also not quite correct to say that this chronicle is not the work of any individual author. Let us see what light its opening verses throw on its contents and author.

Dīpāgamanaṃ Buddhassa dhātu ca[3] *bodhiyāgamaṃ*
saṅgahācariyavādañ[4] *ca dīpamhi sāsanāgamaṃ*
narindāgamanaṃ vaṃsaṃ[5] *kittayissaṃ, suṇātha me.*
pītipāmojjajananaṃ pasādeyyaṃ manoramaṃ
anekākārasampannaṃ cittikatvā suṇātha me.
udaggacittā sumanā pahaṭṭhā tuṭṭhamānasā
niddosaṃ bhadravacanaṃ sakkaccaṃ sampaṭicchatha.
suṇātha sabbe paṇidhāya mānasaṃ, vaṃsaṃ pavakkhāmi paramparāgataṃ[6]
thutippasatthaṃ[7] *bahunābhivaṇṇitaṃ etamhi nānākusumaṃ va ganthitaṃ,*

[1] *Dīpavaṃsa*, edited and translated by Oldenberg, p. 9.
[2] *The Pali Literature of Ceylon*, p. 138.
[3] Variants in the *Vaṃsatthappakāsinī*, p. 36—*dhātūnaṃ, dhātuñ ca.*
[4] „ „ *ibid.*, p. 36, *saṅgahā theravādañ.*
[5] „ „ „ „ *vāsaṃ.*
[6] „ „ „ „ *ābhataṃ.*
[7] „ „ „ „ *atippasatthaṃ.*

anūpamaṃ vaṃsavaraggavāsinaṃ[1] *apubbaṃ anaññaṃ tathasuppakāsitaṃ*[2]
ariyāgataṃ[3] *uttamasabbhi vaṇṇitaṃ suṇātha*[4] *dīpatthuti sādhusakkataṃ.*

'The chronicle of Buddha's coming to the island, the arrival of the relic and the Bo (tree), the collection of the Teacher's words (made at the Councils), the rise of the schools of teachers, the propagation of the religion in the island and the coming of (Vijaya), the chief of men, I am going to narrate, listen to me. Listen attentively to me, (the chronicle which is capable of) generating joy and gladness, (and which is) pleasing and delightful and endowed with various forms. With an elated mind, well pleased, extremely glad (and) with heart's content respectfully accept the faultless (and) good words. Listen all with rapt attention (when) I narrate the chronicle handed down from generation to generation, highly praised, described by many—this being like a garland woven of many kinds of flowers. Listen (when I describe) the eulogy of the island which is honoured by good men—the excellent chronicle of the best and foremost (among the teachers), (which is) new, unrivalled and well set forth, handed down by the elect and praised by those described as the best of the holy ones.'

Here the expression, *suṇātu me*, 'Listen to me', is significant as a form of supplication made by an individual who was in the rôle of the narrator or author of the chronicle. Such is precisely the way in which Mahānāma, the author of the *Mahāvaṃsa*, exhorts the interested hearers, i.e. readers, to hear the chronicle he was going to narrate well. Behind the Pali Canonical expressions, *suṇātu me bhante, suṇantu bhonto mama ekavākyaṃ*, the speaker is a single individual. Thus looked at from this point of view, the *Dīpavaṃsa* is as much the composition of a single author as the *Mahāvaṃsa*, in spite of the fact that the name of the author of the former is yet unknown.

The enumeration of the themes of the *Dīpavaṃsa* in its earlier form is equally important for the reason that it does not take us beyond the establishment of the Buddhist Order in the island by Mahinda and Saṅghamittā. This chronicle in its present form closes, like Mahānāma's great work, with the reign of Mahāsena. The subject matters of its earlier form

---

1 Variants in the *Vaṃsatthappakāsinī*, p. 36, *vādinaṃ*.
2 " " " " *kataṃ suppakāsitaṃ*.
3 " " " " *ariyāgataṃ or ariyābhataṃ*.
4 " " " " *suṇantu*.

first half of the Chapter XVIII and with the verse 44 which reads:

> '*Idāni atthi aññāyo therikā majjhimā navā*
> *vibhajjavādī vinayadharā sāsane paveṇipālakā*
> *bahussutā sīlasampannā obhāsenti mahiṃ iman ti.*'

Here the word *idāni* 'now', which occurs also as the first word of the first verse in the Chapter XVIII is significant. By it the author must have referred to a contemporary state of things.

The mention of the six later Buddhist sects, viz. Hemavatikā, Rājagirikā, Siddhatthā, Pubbaseliyā, Aparaseliyā and Apara Rājagirikā,[1] is also important from the chronological point of view. The Pubbaseliyās and Aparaseliyās do not find mention in any Indian inscription earlier than those of Amarāvatī and Nāgārjunikoṇḍa. The earlier eighteen and these later sects and schools of thought existed also in the time of Buddhaghosa, the author of the *Kathāvatthu Aṭṭhakathā*.[2]

The author of the *Samantapāsādikā* quotes *verbatim* the traditional verses from the *Parivāra* concerning the succession of the Vinaya teachers from Mahinda's time. These are sadly missed in the *Dīpavaṃsa* edited by Oldenberg. But the occurrence of such verses regarding the succession of the Vinaya teachers among the Therīs from Saṅghamittā's time suggests that there were similar verses also regarding the succession of Vinaya teachers among the Theras from Mahinda's time, and it seems quite probable that the verses were quoted in the *Parivāra* from the *Dīpavaṃsa* itself, in which case we have to assume that these were later interpolations in the Vinaya text. If it be so, the *Dīpavaṃsa* as presupposed by the general introduction to the *Vinaya Commentary* must have been concluded with the first half of the Chapter XVIII. This fact may be made clear by a comparison of the succession of the Vinaya Therīs in the *Dīpavaṃsa* with that of the Vinaya Therīs incorporated into the *Parivāra*.

The *Dīpavaṃsa* contains three slightly different traditions regarding Saṅghamittā and the Therīs who accompanied her. According to one[3] Saṅghamittā, Rucānandā, Kanakadattā and Sudhammā were the nuns, each of whom carried a branch of the Bo-tree to the island of Ceylon:

[1] *Dīpavaṃsa*, V, 54.

[2] *Kathāvatthuppakaraṇa-aṭṭhakathā*, *J.P.T.S.*, 1889, pp. 2ff; B. C. Law, *Debates Commentary* (*P.T.S.*), pp. 2ff.

[3] *Dīpavaṃsa*, XVII, vv. 21-22.

Rucānandā Kanakadattā Sudhammā ca mahiddhikā
bahussutā Saṅghamittā chaḷabhiññā vicakkhaṇā
catasso hi bhikkhuṇiyo sabbā ca bodhiṃ āharuṃ.

According to another[1] the Therī Saṅghamittā was accompanied by ten other young nuns, viz. Uttarā, Hemā, Pasādapālā, Aggimittā, Dāsikā, Pheggu, Pabbatā, Mattā, Mallā and Dhammadāsiyā.[2]

According to the third[3] the leading Therīs, Mahādevī, Padumā, Hemāsā, Unnalā, Añjalī and Sumā, accompanied Saṅghamittā, together with sixteen thousand nuns.

It would seem that the third tradition was really about the nuns who flourished not during the reign of king Devānaṃpiya Tissa, the Ceylon contemporary of Asoka, but during that of some other king of Ceylon who came into power after king Duṭṭhagāmaṇi Abhaya and before Kuṭikaṇṇa Tissa.

The three traditions may be reconciled only on the ground that the first of them is concerned with the five Therīs including Saṅghamittā, who were placed in charge of the five Bo-branches, the second with the eleven young nuns of importance including Saṅghamittā, and the third with the six leading Therīs among the many companions of Saṅghamittā.

The *Dīpavaṃsa* while giving an account of the Therīs, first of all, speaks of the well-known Therīs headed by Mahāpajāpatī Gotamī who became well versed in Vinaya (Vinayaññū) in the Master's lifetime. In the second stage it mentions the Therīs, headed by Saṅghamittā, who went to the island of Ceylon in Devānaṃpiya Tissa's time and recited the five Vinaya books and the seven Abhidhamma treatises in Anurādhapura.[4] Immediately after this, it offers a list of the eminent Therīs of the island who were ordained by the Therīs from India and who became noted for their special attainments. The Therīs of Ceylon are connected with the reign of Kākavaṇṇa Tissa and those of the next stage with that of his son and successor Duṭṭhagāmaṇi Abhaya. The Therīs of the next stage are assigned to a period which elapsed after the death of Duṭṭhagāmaṇi, while those of the sixth stage are referred to the time of Vaṭṭagāmaṇi Abhaya. It lists the leading Vinaya Therīs of the island, those connected with the reign of Kuṭikaṇṇa Abhaya and those with the reign of his son and

---

1 *Dīpavaṃsa*, XVIII, vv. 11-12.

2 Again, the list in *Dīpavaṃsa*, XV, vv. 77-78, has Māsagallā for Pasādapālā, Tappā for Pheggu and Mitāvadā for Dāsikā.

3 *Dīpavaṃsa*, XVIII, 24-25.

4 *Ibid.*, XVIII, vv. 11–13.

Vinayaṃ vācayiṃsu piṭakaṃ Anurādhapuravhaye
Vinaye pañca vācesuṃ satta c'eva pakaraṇe. (v. 13.)

successor Bhātiya Abhaya. It should be noted that the last mentioned king finds a respectful mention in the *Samantapāsādikā* in connection with a meeting of the monks called by him for the decision of a Vinaya point then in dispute.[1]

The succession of the Vinaya teachers in the island is traced in the general introduction to the *Samantapāsādikā* from Mahinda and Ariṭṭha to the date of composition of the *Vinaya Commentary*, while that cited from the *Parivāra*, and presumably also from the *Dīpavaṃsa*, leads us to think of nineteen eminent successors of Mahinda. The latter may be taken to bring us as far down as the first or second century A.D.

Thus there is an earlier form of the *Dīpavaṃsa* which was concluded with the reign of Bhātika Abhaya.

It is evident from the prose account in the general introduction to the *Samantapāsādikā* that the *Dīpavaṃsa* presupposed by it contained Chapter XVII giving us an account of the visits of Kakusandha and other previous Buddhas to the island when it was known by other names in succession.

The *Mahārājavaṃsa* giving a genealogy of the Ikṣvāku rulers of the Solar race of Khattiyas from Mahāsammata to Suddhodana, which is now contained in Chapter III, appears to have been a separate chronicle by itself, bodily incorporated into the *Dīpavaṃsa*. The canonical basis of the chronicle may be traced in the legends occurring in the *Pāli Nikāyas* and the *Mahāvastu*. In what stage of the growth of the *Dīpavaṃsa* it came to be included in it we cannot say. The introduction to the *Samantapāsādikā* throws no light on this point.

The traditional succession of the Vinaya teachers in the island of Ceylon, as presented in the *Parivāra*, speaks of twenty-nine generations traced from Mahinda. Unfortunately the later teachers are not connected with the reign of any king. Allowing twenty years for the interval between any two successive generations, it is possible to think that the list brings us down to the first quarter of the fourth century of the Christian era. The kings of Ceylon who find incidental mention in the writings of the great Buddhaghosa and in the *Samantapāsādikā* are none later than Mahānāga or Coranāga, Bhātika, Vāsabha and Sirināga. The career of an eminent Thera called Deva is connected in the *Dīpavaṃsa* with the reign of Tissa, the second son of Sirināga I. If this Thera be no other than the leading Vinaya teacher who figures as the last but one in the above list, it may be concluded that the *Dīpavaṃsa* as known to Buddhaghosa closed with the reign

[1] *Samantapāsādikā*, III, 582-3; cf. *Indian Culture*, Vol. XII, No. 3.

of Sirināga I and his two successors. Its final form, concluded with the reign of Mahāsena, was probably reached in the reign of Dhātusena during which it was caused to be publicly recited.

Let us now see what becomes of the position of the *Dīpavaṃsa* when it is judged by the introductory verses of the *Mahāvaṃsa* which read:

Namassitvāna sambuddhaṃ susuddhaṃ suddhavaṃsajaṃ ।
Mahāvaṃsaṃ pavakkhāmi nānānūnādhikārikaṃ ॥
Porāṇehi kato p'eso atiyitthārito kvaci ।
atīva kvaci saṃkhitto, anekapunaruttako ॥
Vajjitaṃ tehi dosehi sukhaggahaṇadhāraṇaṃ ।
pasādasaṃvegakaraṃ sutito ca upāgataṃ ॥

'Saluting the Supremely Enlightened One, the Pure One, and the Pure-born one, I am narrating the great Chronicle which is not deficient in its many and various themes. This, as composed by the ancients, is in some places very elaborate, in some places very concise, and contains many repetitions. I am narrating the great Chronicle, which is come down by tradition, free from these faults, easy of grasping and understanding, and which generates faith and inspires joy.'

Here the important question is—Does it or does it not mean the Pali *Dīpavaṃsa* by the previous *Mahāvaṃsa* composed by the ancients and presupposed by Mahānāma's *Mahāvaṃsa*? The author of the *Mahāvaṃsa-Ṭīkā* has been at pains to clear up the allusion. He maintains that here Mahānāma refers to the *Aṭṭhakathā Mahāvaṃsa* written in Sinhalese and cherished in the school of Mahāvihāra.[1] But the verses which he quotes in support of his thesis are all from the prologue to the Pali *Dīpavaṃsa* as we now have it.[2] The defects pointed out are all applicable to the same work. Whenever the traditional sayings are quoted in the writings of Buddhaghosa and other Pali commentaries they are all found to be in Pali verse.[3] From the language of the introductory verses of the *Mahāvaṃsa*, it is not at all clear that the allusion is to an earlier form of the Chronicle in a Sinhalese commentary. The work is not claimed to have been a translation from a Sinhalese original.

2. *Aṭṭhakathā Mahāvaṃsa.*—We have seen that an earlier *Mahāvaṃsa* composed by the ancients is presupposed

---

[1] *Vaṃsatthappakāsinī*, I, pp. 35-36.

[2] *Ibid.*, I, p. 48: '*eso Sīhaḷaṭṭhakathā-Mahāvaṃso porāṇehi Sīhaḷāya niruttiyā kato.*'

[3] B. C. Law, *Buddhaghosa*, pp. 45ff.

by the *Mahāvaṃsa* composed in verse by Mahānāma, and that the allusion is evidently to a chronicle of the *Dīpavaṃsa* type. Mahānāma does not refer to any commentary version of the *Mahāvaṃsa* written in Sinhalese, nor does he say that his work was a translation from Sinhalese into Māgadhī meaning Pali. The author of the *Vaṃsatthappakāsinī* has taken a lot of pains to explain the significance of the title of *Mahāvaṃsa* meaning 'The great Chronicle' as well as to enlighten us on the allusion to an earlier chronicle made in the words—*porāṇehi kato p'eso,* 'this as composed by the ancients'. The *Mahāvaṃsa* is the title adopted by Mahānāma for his own work. There was nothing to prevent him from loosely applying the same title to the earlier chronicle *Dīpavaṃsa*. He might easily have got the idea of such a title from a sectional caption, viz., *Mahārājavaṃsa*, used in the *Dīpavaṃsa*, Chapter III. Let us see what the author of the *Mahāvaṃsa Commentary* himself has got to say.[1]

The scholiast has tried with his great erudition to exhaust all probable explanations of the introductory verses of the text. The work is called *Mahāvaṃsa* or 'Great Chronicle' not only due to the fact that it is the chronicle of the great kings and teachers but also because it deals with great themes. This twofold significance of the title is explained in the light of the verses from the prologue to the *Dīpavaṃsa*. The word *dīpatthuti*, literally meaning 'an eulogy of the island', which occurs in these verses, is similarly sought to be explained in the light of other verses from the prologue to the same earlier chronicle. Here these are quoted in the name of 'the Ancients': *Ten'āhu Porāṇā*. But it is not certainly true that these verses testify to the great number of topics dealt with (*saṅkhyāmahattaṃ*). In explaining the significance of the verbal expression *pavakkhāmi*, which literally means 'I will narrate well', the scholiast arbitrarily suggests that by it the author means to say that he was going to narrate the chronicle in the blameless Māgadhī or Pali language, abandoning the Sinhalese diction of the chronicle contained in the *Porāṇatthakathā* as taught in the school of Mahāvihāra. In the sequel, again, two authoritative verses are quoted from the *Dīpavaṃsa*, although in the name of the ancients. Evidently the scholiast has made the confusion between the traditional sayings of the *Porāṇas* in verse and the Sinhalese *Porāṇatthakathā*. It seems rather strange why he, instead of quoting the verses from the *Dīpavaṃsa*, quotes them in the name of the *Porāṇas*. Are we to understand that when the

[1] *Vaṃsatthappakāsinī*, I, pp. 35-36.

Aṭṭhakathā was first written, it was written in Sinhalese? If so, from whom did the inspiration come to write the commentary in Sinhalese in preference to Māgadhī (Pali)?

The *Dīpavaṃsa* presupposes indeed the *Piṭaka* commentaries when it says that king Vaṭṭagāmaṇi caused the *Three Piṭakas* to be committed to writing along with the *Aṭṭhakathās*:

> *Piṭakattayapāliñ ca tassā Aṭṭhakatham pi ca . . .*
> *ciraṭṭhitatthaṃ dhammassa potthakesu likhāpayuṃ.*[1]

This very statement occurs also in the *Mahāvaṃsa.*[2]

But the question still remains—Were these *Aṭṭhakathās* the commentaries written in Sinhalese? As shown elsewhere,[3] there is a commentary process to be noticed throughout the *Three Piṭakas,* in which case the statement, if at all correct, may be taken to mean that the first incentive to producing the commentaries in Sinhalese came from the direction given by Vaṭṭagāmaṇi. Whatever it may be, the traditional sayings of the ancients were all in Pali verses, and none in Sinhalese. The *Mahāvaṃsa-Ṭīkā* speaks, on the other hand, of a *Porāṇaṭṭhakathā* written in Sinhalese prose, in which evidently the Pali sayings of the ancients in verse were quoted. If so, the *Mahāvaṃsa* itself might be a later metrical version of an earlier prose chronicle in Sinhalese prose, but as regards the *Dīpavaṃsa,* it was composed or compiled on the basis of the traditional sayings of the ancients in Pali verse. In such circumstances the *Dīpavaṃsa* must have to be treated as chronologically earlier than the *Aṭṭhakathā Mahāvaṃsa* or the Sinhalese prose chronicle in the *Porāṇaṭṭhakathā* with the traditional Pali verses quoted here and there in the name of the *Porāṇas.*

In support of the statement of the *Mahāvaṃsa-Ṭīkā* regarding the earlier *Aṭṭhakathā Mahāvaṃsa* one may cite the evidence of the Pali commentaries ascribed to Buddhaghosa. One may even go so far as to premise that the general introduction to the *Samantapāsādikā* is only a *verbatim* reproduction in Pali of such an earlier chronicle in a Sinhalese *Aṭṭhakathā.* We have similar reproductions also in the general introduction to the *Sumaṅgalavilāsinī,* the commentary on the *Dīgha Nikāya,* and in those to the *Atthasālinī* and the *Kathāvatthu Aṭṭhakathā.* These reproductions presuppose the *Dīpavaṃsa* and Sinhalese commentaries but nowhere Mahānāma's great work.

---

[1] *Dīpavaṃsa,* XX, 20-21.
[2] *Mahāvaṃsa,* XXXIII, 100-101.
[3] B. C. Law, *Buddhaghosa,* pp. 55ff.

3. *Mahāvaṃsa and Cūḷavaṃsa*.—The *Mahāvaṃsa* proper which is known as the great work of Mahānāma is to be distinguished from its later supplements edited by Geiger under a common title, namely, *Cūḷavaṃsa*. The authors of the supplements applied the title of *Mahāvaṃsa* to their own compositions. Under this very title George Turnour published his edition and translation of the entire work. The relative chronological positions of the chronicle and its supplements may be stated thus: 'The *Mahāvaṃsa* proper with Duṭṭhagāmaṇi as its hero was composed by Mahānāma, the *Cūḷavaṃsa* with Parakkamabāhu the great as its hero was composed by Dhammakitti, the second portion of the *Cūḷavaṃsa* with Kitti-Siri as its hero was composed by Tibboṭuvāve Siddhattha and concluded with a chapter added by Hikkāḍuve Siri Sumaṅgala. A laudable attempt has been made by the Venerable Yagirala Paññānanda to bring it down to modern times.' [1]

(A) *Mahāvaṃsa*:[2] The Sinhalese equivalent of the Pali title of Mahānāma's great work is *Pajjapadoruvaṃsa* (Padyapadoruvaṃsa).[3] It means, according to the *Mahāvaṃsa-Ṭīkā*, that Mahānāma composed this Pali chronicle in verse (padyapadagāthābandhena) on the basis of the *Sīhalaṭṭhakathā-Mahāvaṃsa* of old.[4] The author of the *Ṭīkā* really means that the Mahānāma's composition was an earlier prose chronicle in the *Porāṇaṭṭhakathā* in Sinhalese,[5] which had formed also the basis of the *Abhidhamma* commentaries.

Mahānāma's chronicle is closed, like the *Dīpavaṃsa*, with the reign of Mahāsena. R. Siddhārtha (*I.H.Q.*, VIII, 3, pp. 426ff.) is not right in holding that the Pali *Mahāvaṃsa* (Mahānāma's work) stops abruptly in the middle of the 37th Chapter without concluding it in the usual way. The concluding chapters of the *Dīpavaṃsa* and *Mahāvaṃsa* composed by Mahānāma ended in the same way with the same two reflective verses, if both the works were concluded with an account of the reign of Mahāsena:

'*Asādhusaṃgamen' evaṃ yāvajīvaṃ subhāsubhaṃ*
katvā gato yathākammaṃ so Mahāsenabhūpati.
Tasmā asādhusaṃsaggaṃ ārakā parivajjiya
ahiṃ vāsīvisaṃ khippaṃ kareyy' attahitaṃ budho.'

(*Cūḷavaṃsa*, Chap. 37, vv. 51-52.)

---

[1] B. M. Barua, *Ceylon Lectures*, p. 99.

[2] G. Turnour's Ed. and Eng. Tr., Ceylon, 1837; H. Sumaṅgala and Baṭuwantuḍawe, *Mahāvaṃsa*, Colombo, 1883; Geiger, *Mahāvaṃsa* (*P.T.S.*) and Tr. by him (published by *P.T.S.*); Kambodian Mahāvaṃsa in *J.R.A.S.*, 1902; *J.P.T.S.* (1902-1903); *I.H.Q.*, Vol. VIII, No. 3; Wijesinha, Sinhalese Tr., Colombo, 1889; Eng. Tr. by L. C. Wijesinha, published in 1909.

[3] *Vaṃsatthappakāsini*, II, p. 687. [4] *Ibid.*, I, pp. 41f. [5] *Ibid.*, I, p. 36.

When Mahānāma's work was continued by a later chronicler, Dhammakitti, these two verses occur in the middle of the Chapter 37 instead of at the end. The essential point is that each chapter is expected to conclude with one or more reflective verses. In Chapter 37 of Mahānāma's work the concluding verses were evidently taken from the earlier chronicle. It is justly claimed to have been an improvement on an earlier work. The drawbacks of the earlier work, as pointed out in the introductory verses, are all applicable to the *Dīpavaṃsa.*[1] Comparing the two chronicles, we cannot but come to the conclusion that one is the later remodelled version of the other. A typical example may suffice here to indicate the relation between the two works:

Piṭakattayapāliñ ca tassā aṭṭhakathaṃ pi ca ।
mukhapāṭhena ānesuṃ pubbe bhikkhū mahāmatī ॥
hāniṃ disvāna sattānaṃ tadā bhikkhū samāgatā ।
ciraṭṭhitatthaṃ dhammassa potthakesu likhāpayuṃ ॥

Dīpavaṃsa, XX, 21-22.

Piṭakattayapāliṃ ca tassā aṭṭhakatham pi ca ।
mukhapāṭhena ānesuṃ pubbe bhikkhū mahāmatī ॥
hāniṃ disvāna sattānaṃ tadā bhikkhū samāgatā ।
ciraṭṭhitatthaṃ dhammassa potthakesu likhāpayuṃ ॥

Mahāvaṃsa, XXXIII, 100-101.

In the instance cited above, the same tradition is narrated in two identical Pali verses. But there are certain traditions in the *Mahāvaṃsa* which differ from those in the earlier chronicle, e.g. the legend of Tissarakkhā and last days of Asoka; that of conversion of Asoka to Buddhism by Nigrodha, the posthumous son of Asoka's elder stepbrother Sumana, described as a novice of seven years of age; the description of Suvaṇṇabhūmi as a country on a sea-shore, which was under the sway of a terrible *rākkhasī*. These are all conspicuous by their absence in the earlier chronicle.

The six later Indian Buddhist sects which find mention in the *Dīpavaṃsa* (v. 54) are also found in the general introduction to the *Kathāvatthu Commentary*. They are referred to also in the body of the latter work. The earlier Pali Chronicle is unaware of the two Sinhalese sects, the Dhammarucī and Sāgaliyā, occurring in the *Mahāvaṃsa* (v. 13). They are conspicuous by their absence also in the *Kathāvatthu Aṭṭhakathā* and other works of Buddhaghosa:

---

[1] Geiger, *Dīpavaṃsa and Mahāvaṃsa*, pp. 17ff.

Hemavatikā Rājagirikā Siddhatthā Pubbāparaselikā ı
aparo Rājagiriko chaṭṭhā uppannā aparāparā ‖
Dīpavaṃsa, v. 54.

Hemavatā Rājagiriyā tathā Siddhatthakā pi ca ı
Pubbaseliyabhikkhū ca tathā Aparaseliyā ‖
Vājiriyā, cha ete pi Jambudīpamhi bhinnakā ı
Dhammarucī Sāgaliyā Laṅkādīpamhi bhinnakā ‖
Mahāvaṃsa, vv. 12-13.

The *Mahāvaṃsa* nowhere says how they had originated and when. It speaks indeed of the first development of the Mahāvihāra and the Abhayagirivihāra into two rival schools.[1] The account of their origin is given in the *Mahāvaṃsa-Ṭīkā* and the *Nikāyasaṃgraha*. Both the Pali Chronicles connect the mischievous activities of Mitta, Soṇa and other injudicious persons with the reign of Mahāsena.[2] Judged by the tradition in the earlier Pali Chronicle, the rise of the two Sinhalese sects, called Dhammarucī and Sāgaliyā, occurred in post-Mahāsena times.

The *Mahāvaṃsa* must have obtained the legend of Tissarakkhā and Asoka's last days from an Indian source presupposed by the *Divyāvadāna* narrative of Asoka. We say 'presupposed', because the narrative in the Pali great Chronicle is lacking in the legend of Kuṇāla.[3]

We have so far differed from Oldenberg as to the relative chronological positions of the *Dīpavaṃsa* and the *Sīhalaṭṭhakathā Mahāvaṃsa*. In his opinion, the two works, viz. the *Dīpavaṃsa* and the *Mahāvaṃsa*, were based on the historical introduction to the great commentary of the Mahāvihāra, each of them representing their common subject in its own way, the first work following step by step and almost word for word the traces of the original, the second work proceeding with much greater independence and perfect literary mastery.[4] The position hitherto taken up by us is that the *Dīpavaṃsa*, which is a compilation of the traditional sayings of the ancients in verse, is an earlier work presupposed by the *Porāṇaṭṭhakathā* in Sinhalese, and both of these formed the basis of the *Mahāvaṃsa*. The points of difference between the two Pali Chronicles were due to the reliance placed by the latter work on the traditions recorded in the historical introduction to the Sinhalese commentary.

---

[1] *Mahāvaṃsa*, XXXIII, 96–98.
[2] *Dīpavaṃsa*, XXII, 67–74.
[3] *Mahāvaṃsa*, XX, 2–6.
[4] Oldenberg, *Dīpavaṃsa*, Introduction, p. 7.

The *Mahāvaṃsa-Ṭīkā* speaks of two recensions of the text, namely one belonging to the Mahāvihāra and the other to the Uttaravihāra or Abhayagiri school. It is from this work that we come to know that Thera Mahānāma who resided in a monastery built for him by the commander-in-chief named Dīghasanda, better Dīghasandana, was the author of the *Mahāvaṃsa*.[1] The gifted author himself keeps us entirely in the dark as to his personality and whereabouts. Dīghasandana is traditionally known as a commander-in-chief of Devānampiya Tissa who built a little *pāsāda* on eight pillars for Mahinda, named *Dīghasandasenāpati-pariveṇa* after him.[2] The connection of Mahānāma with this monastery does not, however, enable us to fix the time of the author or the date of the work ascribed to him.

Seeing that both the *Mahāvaṃsa* and the *Dīpavaṃsa*, as we now have them, are concluded alike with an account of the reign of Mahāsena, it may be presumed that the author of the first-named chronicle and that of the concluding portion of the *Dīpavaṃsa* flourished almost in the same age. In the midst of uncertainty, the only traditional basis of chronology is the fact that king Dhātusena (A.D. 460–78) evinced a keen interest in the popularization of the *Dīpavaṃsa*. Dhātusena is the only king of Ceylon after Mahāsena who finds an incidental mention in the *Mahāvaṃsa*. We are told that king Mahāsena caused a monastery, called *Dhātusenapabbata*, to be built in the west of Ceylon.[3] The christening of this Buddhist foundation as *Dhātusenapabbata* in Mahānāma's time is palpably an instance of anachronism but this can surely be construed as a fact, which brings us down to the reign of Dhātusena, who caused the monastery originally built by Mahāsena to be restored in his time and named after him. It is equally important to note that the annual Mahinda festival was chosen by the king as the fittest occasion for the edification of the chronicle of the island of Ceylon.

The Thera Mahānāma of the Dīghasandana or Dīghāsana monastery, to whom the *Mahāvaṃsa Ṭīkā* ascribes the *Mahāvaṃsa*, appears to have been no other person than the Thera Mahānāma to whom king Moggallāna I (A.D. 496–513), the younger son of Dhātusena, dedicated the *Pabbatavihāra*

[1] *Vaṃsatthappakāsinī*, II, p. 687:

Dīghasandasenāpatinā kārāpitamahāpariveṇavāsinā Mahānāmo ti garūhi gahitanāmadheyyena therena . . . katassa Padyapadoruvaṃsassa.

[2] *Mahāvaṃsa*, XV, 212f.; *Cūlavaṃsa*, XXXVIII, 16.

[3] *Mahāvaṃsa*, XXXVII, 42: *pacchimāyaṃ Dhātusenapabbataṃ ca akārayi.*

built by him.[1] On reading between the lines, it becomes apparent that the Thera was a resident of the Dīghasandana monastery previous to this dedication and was, therefore, connected more with the reign of Dhātusena.[2] Mahānāma is described as the maternal uncle of Dhātusena according to the *Cūḷavaṃsa*. Dhātusena in his early life was initiated as a novice by his maternal uncle who was then a Thera in the Dīghasandana monastery.[3]

The encouragement given by king Dhātusena for the edification of the *Dīpavaṃsa* must have served as a great impetus to the composition of the *Mahāvaṃsa* or *Padyapadoruvaṃsa* in Pali. The writing of a *Dīpavaṃsa-Aṭṭhakathā* may have resulted from the same literary process. At all events the mention in the *Mahāvaṃsa* of a *Pabbatavihāra* named after Dhātusena, its restorer, is a fact, which must have an important bearing on the question of the date of its composition.

The date of composition of Mahānāma's chronicle thus arrived at from an internal evidence gives rise to an important question whether Mahānāma's work was concluded with the reign of Mahāsena or it included the whole of the Chapter 37 which now occurs partly in the *Mahāvaṃsa* proper and partly in the *Cūḷavaṃsa*. To assume that Mahānāma's work had ended as in Geiger's edition is to admit that it ended abruptly without its usual reflective verses. It is true that the text of Mahānāma's work as in Geiger's edition was precisely before the author of the *Vaṃsatthappakāsinī*. If the later composer Dhammakitti continued the chronicle in his own way, there is apparently no reason why he should have extended the Chapter 37 instead of beginning with a new chapter. The date suggested in Mahānāma's work itself leads us to think that it was concluded with an account of the reign of Dhātusena. In other words Mahānāma's chronicle consisted not of 37 chapters but of 38.

(B) *Cūḷavaṃsa:* The Thera Dhammakitti is traditionally known as the author of the first portion of the *Cūḷavaṃsa*

[1] *Cūḷavaṃsa*, XXXIX, 42:

Pabbataṃ tu vihāraṃ so katvā therassa dāpayi ।
Mahānāmasanāmassa Dīghāsanavihārake ॥

[2] This important point is missed by both E. W. Adikaram (*Early History of Buddhism in Ceylon*, p. 9) and G. C. Mendis (The Pali Chronicles of Ceylon, *University of Ceylon Review*, Vol. IV, No. 2, pp. 20ff.).

[3] *Cūḷavaṃsa*, XXXVIII, pp. 16-17:

Mātu sodariyo tesaṃ saddho pabbajja vattati ।
Dīghasandakatāvāse, Dhātuseno pi māṇavo ॥
santike tassa pabbajja rukkhamūlaṃhi ekadā ।

representing a continuation of the *Mahāvaṃsa proper*. According to Sinhalese tradition, Dhammakitti was a Burmese monk who came to Ceylon during the reign of king Parakkamabāhu II in the thirteenth century A.D.[1]

Geiger notices a turning point in the chronicle of the later kings of Ceylon immediately after the description of the reign of Parakkamabāhu I. Thus the first supplement to Mahānāma's great work may be taken to have comprised forty-three chapters (XXXVII–LXXIX).

In the *Cūḷavaṃsa* itself we have no mention of any Burmese Thera known by the name of Dhammakitti and connected with the reign of Parakkamabāhu I. We have, on the other hand, the mention in it (LXXVI, 32) of a Ceylonese Thera, called Dhammakitti, who was deputed by Parakkamabāhu I as one of the envoys to the then king of Rāmañña, Lower Burma. The *Cūḷavaṃsa* (LXXXIV, 11) eloquently speaks of the great qualities of a leading Colian Thera known by the same name who came across to Ceylon on an invitation from king Parakkamabāhu II to effect a thorough reform of the *Saṅgha*. It is difficult to say if he was the author of the first supplement. The consensus of opinion, however, is in favour of regarding him as the monk who wrote the account in the *Mahāvaṃsa* from the reign of Mahāsena to that of Parakkamabāhu II.[2]

The second portion of the *Cūḷavaṃsa* may be taken to comprise eleven chapters (LXXX–XC). It presents a chronicle of kings from the reign of Vijayabāhu II to that of Parakkamabāhu IV (*circa* A.D. 1300).[3] The identity of the author of this supplement is still unknown. It would seem possible that this was the composition of the erudite Colian Mahāthera, a master of different languages, who came to Ceylon on an invitation from king Parakkamabāhu IV (A.D. 1325–1347 ?).

The third portion (Chs. 91 to 100) brings the chronicle down to the reign of Kitti-Siri-Rājasīha (A.D. 1767–1782), the last independent king of Ceylon. The Thera Tibboṭuvāve Sumaṅgala is traditionally known as its author, while the concluding chapter bringing the history of Ceylon down to A.D. 1815 was added by Hikkaḍuve Siri-Sumaṅgala.[4]

In adopting the title of *Cūḷavaṃsa* for the continuation of Mahānāma's work Geiger seeks to justify it on two authorities: (1) a statement in the *Cūḷavaṃsa*, Chapter 99,

---

1 *Cūḷavaṃsa*, edited by Geiger, Introduction, p. iii.
2 *J.R.A.S.*, 1896, pp. 202ff.
3 Geiger, *Cūḷavaṃsa*, Introduction, p. iv.
4 Malalasekera, *Dictionary*, *sub voce Cūḷavaṃsa*, I, p. 901.

v. 76, and (2) a statement in the Sinhalese Rājāvalīya.[1] The two statements are found on a proper examination to be of the same import. Both propose to divide the kings of Ceylon into those of the *Mahāvaṃsa* meaning the great dynasty and those of the *Cūḷavaṃsa*, i.e. the lesser dynasty. According to the Rājāvalīya the line of the kings of the first dynasty ended with Mahāsena, and the line of the kings of the later dynasty began with Kitti-Siri-Meghavaṇṇa, the son of Mahāsena. The later dynasty is called Cūḷa or lesser or lower because the pedigree of the kings belonging to it is heterogeneous, being an intermingling between the descendants of those monarchs who brought to the island the sacred Bo-Branch, and those who brought the tooth relic. But this division of the kings of Ceylon cannot be taken as an evidence to prove that the chronicle composed by Mahānāma had ended with the reign of Mahāsena. Here we must bear in mind also the fact that the *Dīpavaṃsa* applies the name of *Mahārājavaṃsa* only to the Indian kings of the solar race descended from Mahāsammata and Okkāka.

(C) *Uttaravihāra Mahāvaṃsa:* The *Mahāvaṃsa Ṭīkā* expressly refers to an Uttaravihāra or Abhayagiri version of the *Mahāvaṃsa* which differed in some respects from the Mahāvihāra recension. Just one instance of difference between the two recensions is cited in the *Ṭīkā*,[2] but there might have been other instances as well, which may be detected in the light of the difference between the two commentaries produced in the two schools, both in Sinhalese. The instance cited in the *Ṭīkā* is concerned apparently with what is called *Mahārājavaṃsa* in the *Dīpavaṃsa*.

4. *Dīpavaṃsa Aṭṭhakathā*.—In two contexts[3] the *Mahāvaṃsa Ṭīkā* has quoted the views of a *Dīpavaṃsa* commentary, written probably in Sinhalese. When this was written and by whom—all these are not known. None need be surprised if the writing of this commentary resulted from the encouragement given by king Dhātusena for the improvement of the *Dīpavaṃsa*.

5. *Mahāvaṃsa Aṭṭhakathās*.—The *Mahāvaṃsa Ṭīkā* has cited the authority of the Sinhalese commentaries on the *Mahāvaṃsa*, one belonging to the Mahāvihāra and the other to the Uttaravihāra or Abhayagiri. The latter contained

---

[1] *Cūḷavaṃsa* (Geiger's Ed.), Introduction, pp. 1ff.

[2] *Vaṃsatthappakāsinī*, I, p. 134: *Uttaravihāravāsīnaṃ pana Mahāvaṃse: Sīhassararañño puttapaputtakā dvāsīti-sahassāni rājāno ahesuṃ, tesaṃ kaṇiṭṭhako Bhagusakko nāma rājā, tassa puttapaputtakā dvāsīti-sahassāni rājāno ahesuṃ, tesaṃ kaṇiṭṭhako Jayaseno ti vuttaṃ.*

[3] *Ibid.*, II, pp. 411, 683.

certain legends, however few, which were not to be found in the former.[1] Some of the additional matters supplied in the Uttaravihāra commentary have been utilized in the *Mahābodhivaṃsa*, the *Mahāvaṃsa Ṭīkā* and the *Extended Mahāvaṃsa*.

The *Mahāvaṃsa Ṭīkā* presupposes two other earlier commentaries, namely, one by Pāsāṇadīpavāsī Upatissa Thera and the other known as the *Gaṇṭhipadavaṇṇanā*.

6. *Mahābodhivaṃsakathā*.—This is another older work which is quoted by name in the *Mahāvaṃsa Ṭīkā*. The Pali verse which is cited from this work cannot, however, be traced in the *Mahābodhivaṃsa* edited by Arthur Strong for the Pali Text Society:

> *Mahābodhiṃ pūjissanti Laṅke'tasmiṃ narādhipā*
> *paccatthikā na hiṃseyyuṃ-esā sambodhidhammatā.*[2]

By the title, *Mahābodhivaṃsakathā*, Malalasekera rightly understands a *Mahābodhivaṃsa Aṭṭhakathā*.[3] The question is—is the older work presupposed by the *Mahāvaṃsa Ṭīkā* to be identified with the Pali version of the *Mahābodhivaṃsa* now extant or should it be identified with its earlier Sinhalese form? There is no consensus of opinion as yet on this point. Geiger admits the possibility of the work being 'identical with the *Mahābodhivaṃsa*, still in existence',[4] while Malalasekera doubts it. The latter is inclined to think that careful perusal of both the *Mahābodhivaṃsa* and the *Mahāvaṃsa Ṭīkā* shows that the *Mahābodhivaṃsa*, at least from the point of view of its language, is later than the *Mahāvaṃsa Ṭīkā*.[5]

It is certain that although the Pali version is distinctly given the name of *Mahābodhivaṃsa*, it is, in fact, written in the style of a commentary, with the usual introductory verse:

> *Ken'aṭṭhena mahābodhi, kassa sambandhinī ca sā?*
> *kiṃ sādhinī abhitthutā, kena kattha-ppatiṭṭhitā?*[6]

The Pali version is claimed to have been a composition of the author on the basis of an older form written by the previous teachers in the Sinhalese idiom for the benefit of the people of Ceylon.[7]

Geiger rightly points out that the verses in the Pali *Mahābodhivaṃsa* are all taken from the *Mahāvaṃsa*. Its

---

1 *Vaṃsatthappakāsinī*, I, pp. 125, 155, 177, 187, 247, 249, 289, 290.
2 *Ibid.*, II, p. 412.
3 *Ibid.*, II, p. 412.
4 Geiger, *The Dīpavaṃsa and Mahāvaṃsa*, p. 49.
5 *Vaṃsatthappakāsinī*, I, Introduction, p. cvii.
6 *Mahābodhivaṃsa*, p. 1.
7 *Pubbācariyakesarihi Laṅkāvāsinaṃ atthāya Sīhalabhāsāya ṭhapitaṃ Mahābodhivaṃsaṃ ahaṃ idāni avasesa-desavāsinaṃ subodhaṃ karonto . . . Māgadhābhidhānāya . . . vācāya racayanto . . . Mahābodhivaṃsa*, p. 1.

direct dependence on the *Samantapāsādikā* cannot be doubted. The *Jātakaṭṭhakathā* in its present form is clearly presupposed.[1]

It may be important, while discussing the date of composition of the *Mahābodhivaṃsa* in its Pali form, to note that the work was indebted to the Mahāvihāra version of the older *Mahāvaṃsa Aṭṭhakathā* in Sinhalese for the names of Kālāsoka's ten sons,[2] and to the Uttaravihāra or Abhayagiri version of the same for the names of the nine Nanda brothers,[3] but not to the Sinhalese *Mahābodhivaṃsakathā*.

It does not seem possible that there was a text known by the name of *Mahābodhivaṃsa* other than the *Mahābodhivaṃsakathā* which, when first written, was written in the style of a commentary.

The *Gandhavaṃsa* mentions the *Bodhivaṃsa* along with the *Dīpavaṃsa*, the *Cullavaṃsa*, the *Mahāvaṃsa* and the *Paṭisambhidāmagga Aṭṭhakathā*, and includes Upatissa among the Sinhalese teachers. In the *Sāsanavaṃsadīpa*, on the other hand, Upatissa is definitely mentioned as the author of the *Bodhivaṃsa*. It is said that Upatissa undertook to compose the work at the instance of the Thera Dāṭhānāga. One Thera Dāṭhānāga finds respectful mention in the *Cūḷavaṃsa* (LIV, 36) as a contemporary of king Mahinda IV (A.D. 956–72), but the connection of Upatissa, to whom the *Sāsanavaṃsadīpa* ascribes the *Bodhivaṃsa*, remains hypothetical. One may agree with Geiger if the Sinhalese *Mahābodhivaṃsakathā* be regarded as a work written in the last quarter of the tenth century, leaving the question of the date of composition of the Pali work still open.

7. *Mahācetiyavaṃsa Aṭṭhakathā.*—It is particularly in connection with the Mahāthūpa or Great Dagoba built by king Duṭṭhagāmaṇi that the *Mahāvaṃsa Ṭīkā* refers us for certain important details to an older work, mentioned in one context by the name of the *Mahācetiyavaṃsa Aṭṭhakathā*,[4] and in a second context by that of the *Cetiyavaṃsa Aṭṭhakathā*.[5] Just as by the *Bodhivaṃsa* and *Mahābodhivaṃsa* the one and the same chronicle is meant, so by the *Cetiyavaṃsa Aṭṭhakathā* and *Mahācetiyavaṃsa Aṭṭhakathā* was presumably meant one and the same chronicle—the chronicle of the *thūpas*. Geiger[6] rightly observes that the *Cetiyavaṃsa Aṭṭhakathā* was clearly

---

[1] Geiger, *op. cit.*, pp. 75ff.

[2] *Mahābodhivaṃsa*, p. 98; *Vaṃsatthappakāsinī*, I, p. 177: *Kālāsokassa atrajaputtā dasabhātukā ahesuṃ. Tesaṃ pana nāmaṃ Aṭṭhakathāyaṃ vuttaṃ.*

[3] *Ibid.*, p. 98; *Vaṃsatthappakāsinī*, I, p. 177: *tesaṃ navannaṃ uppattikkamañ ca Uttaravihāraṭṭhakathāyaṃ vuttaṃ.*

[4] *Vaṃsatthappakāsinī*, II, p. 509.

[5] *Ibid.*, II, p. 548.

[6] Geiger, *op. cit.*, p. 49.

a work on the dagobas of Ceylon. It is to be expected therefore that it stands in closer relation to the *Thūpavaṃsa*. The *Mahāvaṃsa Ṭīkā* admits at the place where it speaks of the *Cetiyavaṃsa Aṭṭhakathā* that the description of the *Vessantara Jātaka* and the *Abhinikkhamaṇa* in the Dhātugabbha of the Mahāthūpa is here given in detail. The pictorial decoration of the relic cell in the Ruvanaveḷi Dagoba is in fact fully described in the *Thūpavaṃsa*. The *Mahācetiyavaṃsa Aṭṭhakathā* seems to treat especially of the history of the Mahāthūpa built by Duṭṭhagāmaṇi.

Here, precisely as in the case of the *Mahābodhivaṃsakathā*, we are not to suppose that the work, in spite of its being given the name of a commentary, was preceded by a text called *Cetiyavaṃsa* or *Mahācetiyavaṃsa*. It probably served as a commentary to the *Mahāvaṃsa* description of the dagobas built in India and Ceylon. This was written in Sinhalese and served as the authoritative basis of the Pali *Thūpavaṃsa*.

8. *Vaṃsatthappakāsinī*.[1]—This title is employed in Burmese manuscripts for the Pali commentary on the *Mahāvaṃsa*, while its author himself suggests the double title of *Vaṃsatthappakāsinī* and *Padyapadoruvaṃsassa atthavaṇṇanā*.[2] In the Kambodian MSS., however, the work bears the name of *Aṭṭhakathā Mahāvaṃsa*, meaning an Exegetical Chronicle. According to a tradition current in Ceylon, the author of the commentary, too, was a Thera named Mahānāma. Turnour who recorded this tradition was wrongly led to think that probably the author of the text and the author of the commentary were one and the same person. That they were two different persons separated by a considerable interval of time may now be taken for granted.

The scholiast, Mahānāma or whoever else he might have been, often respectfully refers to the author of the text as *ācariya*. He is acquainted not only with the two recensions of the text, *viz*. the Mahāvihāra and the Abhayagiri, but also with two different Sinhalese commentaries produced in the two rival schools. He is aware of the variants in the texts presented before him. Among other older works in Sinhalese availed of by him include a *Dīpavaṃsa Aṭṭhakathā*, an *Exegetical Mahābodhivaṃsa* and an *Exegetical Mahācetiyavaṃsa*.

Malalasekera has drawn our attention to the Bodhgayā inscription of the Thera Mahānāma in which the succession of six Theras of Ceylon is traced through Bhara, Rāhula, Upasena (I), Mahānāma (I), Upasena (II) and Mahānāma (II),

[1] Malalasekera has edited it for the P.T.S. in two parts.
[2] G. P. Malalasekera, *Vaṃsatthappakāsinī*, I, Introduction, p. vii.

the last-named Thera being the author of the epigraph. Apart from other cogent details, this is nothing but a string of names without any bearing on the author of the *Mahāvaṃsa Ṭīkā* or his time.[1]

The compliment paid to Dhātusena for certain pious constructions may be interesting as suggesting that the work could not have been written previous to the reign of this king.[2] This does not, however, lead us very far towards the solution of the problem, the name of Dhātusena occurring as well in the *Mahāvaṃsa* itself.[3]

The change of certain place-names noticed in the commentary, *e.g.* that of the Issarasamaṇārāma into Kassapagiri-vihāra, with Kassagiri, Kaṇḍagiri, Kandaragiri, Kassakagiri or Vessagiri as its variants, or that of Sāmagalla into Moragalla, is not a decisive fact at all.

There is no better way of fixing the date of compilation of the *Mahāvaṃsa Ṭīkā* than one suggested by Geiger. In the first place the reference made to Bhāgineyya-Dāṭhopatissa who is no other than Dāṭhopatissa II (A.D. 664–73) helps us to fix the upper limit. As for the lower limit, one may take these two facts into consideration: (1) that the author of the commentary is unaware of the *Extended Mahāvaṃsa* and the first supplement to the *Mahāvaṃsa* by Dhammakitti; (2) that it is utilized in the Pali *Thūpavaṃsa* composed in the middle of the thirteenth century and must therefore have been earlier than the latter. These facts have led Geiger to place the date of compilation of the *Ṭīkā* between A.D. 1000 and 1250.

9. *Dāṭhāvaṃsa*.[4]—This is the abbreviated title for the Pali chronicle which was known to Dhammakitti, the author of the first part of the *Cūḷavaṃsa* by the name of *Dāṭhādhātu-vaṃsa*[5] and which was intended by its author to be called *Jinadantadhātuvaṃsa*.[6] The shorter title, *Dāṭhāvaṃsa*, is adopted in the *Gandhavaṃsa* and *Sāsanavaṃsa*. The Thera Dhammakitti is rightly credited with the authorship of the Pali chronicle in its present form in the last-named two Pali works written in Burma. The name of Dhammakitti is fittingly mentioned in the closing verses of the work as its illustrious author. In them, he is described as a pupil of the

[1] *Vaṃsatthappakāsinī*, I, Introduction, pp. civff.
[2] *Ibid.*, II, p. 626. [3] *Mahāvaṃsa*, XXXVII, 42.
[4] Vide *J.P.T.S.*, 1886; Devanāgarī Ed. and Tr. by B. C. Law, 1925; *J.B.B.R.A.S.*, XI, 1875; *J.A.S.B.*, 1837; English Tr. by Coomaraswamy, 1874; *Academy*, Sept. 1874; C. Swamy's Ed. in Sinhalese character; '*Le Dāṭhāvança: On Histoire de la dent relique du Buddha Gotama*', 1884.
[5] *Cūḷavaṃsa*, XXXVII, 93: *Dāṭhādhātussa vaṃsamhi*.
[6] *Dāṭhāvaṃsa*, I, 10; colophon 4.

worthy pupil of the Thera Sāriputta and as the well-known author of a *Ṭīkā* (*Sāratthadīpanī*) on the *Vinaya Commentary* called *Samantapāsādikā*, a *Ṭīkā* on the *Aṅguttara Commentary* (*Manorathapūraṇī*), a Ṭīkā on the *Candra-vyākaraṇa* called the *Candrapañcikā*, a Pāṇinian treatise on Sanskrit grammar by Candragomin, and a Vinaya compendium known by the name of the *Vinayasaṅgraha*. He is praised as one of the most erudite scholars who was well-versed in the *Tarkaśāstra* (systems of Logic) and a master of the doctrine of the Buddha. He was appointed to the coveted office of a *Rājaguru* (Royal Preceptor) by the reigning king Parakkamabāhu, evidently through the influence of his queen Līlāvatī. The chronicle was written at the instance of Parakkama, then the commander-in-chief of Ceylon, who placed Līlāvatī on the vacant throne of the island.[1] Parakkamabāhu, the husband of Līlāvatī III, was no other than king Parakkamabāhu I (A.D. 1197–1200). Geiger rightly opines that the Pali Dāṭhāvaṃsa must have been written shortly after Līlāvatī was raised to the throne in A.D. 1211.[2]

Going by Dhammakitti's own statement, we cannot but admit that his metrical history of the Buddha's tooth-relic was based on an older work in Sinhalese. When this older work was written and by whom is still a matter of speculation. That the Sinhalese original too, was a metrical composition, may be easily inferred from the following description which occurs in Chapter I, verse 10:

> *Sadesabhāsāya kavīhi Sīhale katam pi vaṃsaṃ Jinadanta-dhātuyā.*

According to tradition, the Sinhalese original known as *Daḷadāvaṃsa* was written in 845 B.E. and during the reign of Kitti-Siri-Meghavaṇṇa (A.D. 344–362). Kern wrongly calculated this traditional date of composition to be about 310 A.D.[3]; he could have made out 362 A.D. to be the required date by deducting 483, which was the initial year of the Buddha Era current in Ceylon up till the fifteenth century. But the question arises, is this authentic at all?

The case may be argued thus: We cannot think of a Sinhalese chronicle of the Buddha's tooth-relic before its arrival in the island during the reign of Kitti-Siri-Meghavaṇṇa. Secondly the *Dāṭhādhātuvaṃsa* finds mention in the *Cūḷavaṃsa* (37, 93) in connection with the reign of Kitti-Siri-Megavaṇṇa.

1 *Dāṭhāvaṃsa*, I, 4–10.
2 Geiger, *Dīpavaṃsa and Mahāvaṃsa*, p. 79.
3 *Manual of Indian Buddhism*, p. 89, f.n. 1.

Dāṭhādhātussa vaṃsamhi vuttassa vidhinā sa taṃ |
gahetvā bahumānena katvā sammānaṃ uttamaṃ ||

which may be rendered:

'Receiving it (the tooth-relic) with great honour and doing it the best kind of honour in accordance with the prescribed rule as described in the *Dāṭhādhātuvaṃsa*.'

But reading between the lines, one cannot fail to notice that the statement does not prove at all the date of composition of the Sinhalese original. The Pali chronicle was well-known in Ceylon in the time of Dhammakitti, the author of the first part of the *Cūḷavaṃsa*. All that he wants to say is that the mode of worship of the tooth-relic followed by Kitti-Siri-Meghavaṇṇa was similar to the description in the *Dāṭhāvaṃsa* then known to him.

Geiger points out that the Sinhalese *Daladāpūjāvalī* is a later compilation, which closely follows the narrative of the Pali *Dāṭhāvaṃsa*.

Lastly, if the Pali version were a faithful reproduction of the older Sinhalese work, its artificial *kāvya* style alone would have sufficed to place its date of composition after the *Mahāvaṃsa*.

10. *Thūpavaṃsa*.—This is the improved Pali version of the traditional history of the Thūpas in India and Ceylon built up till the reign of king Duṭṭhagāmaṇi of Ceylon, the term *thūpa* meaning a dagoba or relic-shrine (*dhātu-cetiya*). Strictly speaking, the description given was meant for the Mahāthūpa caused to be built by king Duṭṭhagāmaṇi at Anurādhapura, the traditional account of other *thūpas* being given by the way:

Yasmiṃ sayiṃsu jina-dhātuvarā samantā,
chabbaṇṇa-raṃsi visarehi samujjalantā;
nimmāya loka-hita-hetu janassa rūpaṃ,
taṃ thūpaṃ abbhūtatamaṃ sirasā namitvā.[1]

In the colophon, too, the chronicle is described as *Thūpavarassa vaṃso*, 'The history of the Great Thūpa'.

The author of this version of the Pali *Thūpavaṃsa* is introduced in the colophon as the Thera Vācissara who was appointed by king Parakkamabāhu to the office of the Librarian of the Royal Library (Dhammāgāra). He is also described as the author of the *Līnatthadīpanī Ṭīkā*, a sub-commentary on the *Paṭisambhidāmagga*, the *Saccasaṅkhepa-atthadīpanā* and the *Visuddhimaggasaṅkhepa-atthappakāsinī*.

---

[1] *Thūpavaṃsa*, edited by B. C. Law, p. 1.

In the *Cūḷavaṃsa*, the same Thera Vācissara finds mention as the leading Thera of the island of Laṅkā of his time, who lived in the time of king Vijayabāhu III, father of Parakkamabāhu II. Vācissara led the deputation of the Theras of Ceylon sent to the kingdoms of Pāṇḍya and Coḷa for the search of the Buddha's tooth-relic and bowl.[1]

According to the colophon, Vācissara undertook to compile the *Dhātuvaṃsa* at the instance of a Venerable Thera who made the request to him while he was staying at the Mahindasena monastery. The ṇame of the supplicant is not, however, given.

The Pali *Thūpavaṃsa*[2] in its present form presupposes an older Pali version and a still older Sinhalese version. There are a few minor points of disagreement between the Sinhalese *Thūpavaṃsa* and Vācissara's chronicle. Unfortunately the names of the authors of the Sinhalese *Thūpavaṃsa* and the older Pali version are unknown. The *Extended Mahāvaṃsa* expressly mentions the *Buddhavaṃsa*, the *Mahāvaṃsa*, the *Līnattha* and the *Thūpavaṃsa* as previous authorities on which its history was based.[3] This *Thūpavaṃsa* must have been an older work, inasmuch as the *Līnattha* (*Līnatthadīpanī*) is evidently a sub-commentary on the *Paṭisambhidāmagga*.

11. *Hatthavanagallavihāravaṃsa*.—This, as its name implies, is a Pali traditional history of the Hatthavanagalla monastery erected by Goṭhābhaya-Meghavaṇṇa and repaired by Parakkamabāhu II. The monastery is said to have been built on the spot where king Siri-Saṅghabodhi gave away his head to a poor man. The chronicle which was written in the middle of the thirteenth century[4] offers us a full account of the life of Sirisaṅghabodhi.

12. *Nalāṭadhātuvaṃsa*.—This is the Pali original of the Sinhalese *Dhātuvaṃsa* written by the Thera Kakusandha. The name and age of the author of this chronicle are as yet unknown.[5]

13. *Later Sinhalese Chronicles*.—Now turning to the later chronicles written in Sinhalese, we have got to consider the chronological position of the *Thūpavaṃsa*, *Pūjāvalī*,

[1] *Cūḷavaṃsa*, LXXXI, 20–23.

[2] Vide *P.T.S. Ed.* by B. C. Law (1935); *Sinhalese Ed.* by Dhammaratana, 1896; *J.R.A.S.*, 1898; *English Tr.* by B. C. Law (*Legend of the Topes*, *Bibliotheca Indica* Series, 1945).

[3] G. P. Malalasekera, *Extended Mahāvaṃsa* (Royal Asiatic Society, Ceylon Branch), XXXVIII, 15.

[4] Wickremasinghe, *Catalogue of Sinhalese Manuscripts*, pp. 70-71.

[5] Geiger, *Dīpavaṃsa and Mahāvaṃsa*, p. 91.

Daladāpūjāvalī, *Dhātuvaṃsa*, *Nikāyasaṅgraha*, *Rājaratnākara* and *Rājāvalī*.

(*a*) *Thūpavaṃsa:* As compared with the Pali version of this chronicle, its Sinhalese version contains more details, and may, in many respects, be regarded as an extended paraphrase of the former. But it seems that the author of the Sinhalese work made also use of the older Sinhalese history of the dagoba on which the Pali version was based. 'The *Jātaka Nidānakathā* is here also used as the basis for the introduction, the *Samantapāsādikā* for the history of Asoka and the missions sent out under him, especially that of Mahinda and the *Mahāvaṃsa* for the rest. Unquestionably the *Mahāvaṃsa Ṭīkā* was also made use of occasionally.' These facts have led Geiger to conclude that if the Pali *Thūpavaṃsa* were written in about 1250, the later Sinhalese version of the chronicle must have been produced shortly after that, and shortly before 1260 A.D.

(*b*) *Pūjāvalī:* The Thera Mayūrapāda is known as the author of the *Pūjāvalī*, who was a contemporary of the Thera Dhammakitti, the author of the first supplement to the *Mahāvaṃsa*. Mayūrapāda may accordingly be assigned to the second half of the thirteenth century.[1]

(*c*) *Daḷadā Pūjāvalī:* This is the Sinhalese version of the history of the tooth-relic which closely follows the text of the Pali *Dāṭhāvaṃsa*. The name of Parakkamabāhu IV is mentioned among the princes noted for the homage paid to the tooth-relic. This Parakkamabāhu who ascended the throne in about 1325 A.D. is said to have written the Dāṭhādhātucāritta, a Sinhalese work on the ceremonial of the tooth-relic.[2] It seems most probable that the *Daḷadā Pūjāvalī* was written in the reign of this king who is referred to in the work as '*apage Siri-Parākramabāhu*', our (king) Siri-Parākramabāhu.[3]

(*d*) *Dhātuvaṃsa:* The Sinhalese *Dhātuvaṃsa* written by the Thera Kakusandha is evidently a faithful paraphrase of the Pali *Nalāṭa-dhātuvaṃsa*. There is no certainty as yet about the age in which Kakusandha lived and wrote his work.

(*e*) *Nikāyasaṅgraha:* It is a traditional history of Buddhism in India and Ceylon written by the Mahāthera Jayabāhu surnamed Devarakkhita who was famous as Dharmakīrti with special reference to the Buddhist sects. His teacher, Dharmakīrti, was an illustrious monk who caused to be built a vihāra called Saddhammatilaka in the village

---

[1] Geiger, *op. cit.*, pp. 88ff.

[2] Malalasekera, *Dictionary*, II, p. 151.

[3] Geiger, *op. cit.*, p. 82.

known by the name of Gaḍalādeṇiya when king Bhuvanekabāhu was reigning in the city of Gaṅgasiripura. The chronicle was written in the reign of Vīrabāhu II. The *Nikāyasaṅgraha* tells us that in the twentieth year of the reign of Bhuvanekabāhu V (A.D. 1396), his cousin, prince Vīrabāhu became king, most probably of the central part of Ceylon, as Vīrabāhu II. It places the accession of king Parākramabāhu II in 1809 B.E. or A.D. 1266. It tells us also that Alakeswara, evidently a minister to king Bhuvanekabāhu V, was the builder of the new Jayavardhanapura on the site of a village called Daragamuwa (Dvāragāma).[1]

(*f*) *Saddharmaratnākara:* It is another traditional history of Buddhism written in Sinhalese shortly after the period represented by the *Nikāyasaṅgraha*. A clear idea of its date of composition may be gathered from the fact that in it Vīrabāhu is said to have been preceded in his office by his brother Vīra Alakeswara, and earlier by a son of Alakeswara the Viceroy. Vīrabāhu was succeeded in his office by two others previous to the return of his brother, Vīra Alakeswara from India. According to the *Saddharmaratnākara* his successor was a prince of the Mehenavaravaṃsa and was Epāṇa, a fact which finds its corroboration in the Chinese chronicles stating that Vīrabāhu was succeeded on the throne by his son Parākramabāhu Epāṇa meaning Parākramabāhu VI.[2]

(*g*) *Attanagaluvaṃsa:* This is the Sinhalese translation of a Pali work, *Attanogaruvaṃsa*, which was dedicated to the General Satrusinha Kuñjara, brother of Alakeswara, prime minister to king Bhuvanekabāhu V. The *Mayūrasandesa* was a contemporary Sinhalese poem in which both king Bhuvanekabāhu V and his viceroy Alakeswara find an incidental mention.[3]

(*h*) *Rājaratnākara:* It contains a traditional history of the kings of ancient India and Ceylon written by Walgampoya Terunnanse probably in about the middle of the sixteenth century. There are reasons to believe that the author of this Sinhalese chronicle made use of both the *Pūjāvalī* and the *Nikāyasaṅgraha*.[4]

(*i*) *Rājāvalī:* This is the latest known traditional history of the kings of ancient India and Ceylon which as a whole may be treated as the work of a single individual. The fact

[1] *Nikāyasaṅgraha*, translated by C. M. Fernando, pp. xivff.
[2] *Ibid.*, Introduction, p. xviii.
[3] Fernando, *op. cit.*, Introduction, p. xvi.
[4] Geiger, *op. cit.*, pp. 95ff.

that its account closes with the reign of Vimala Dhamma Suriya (A.D. 1679–1701) has led Geiger to take it to be a compilation of the beginning of the eighteenth century.[1]

14. *Vuttamālā.*—This is a Pali poem written in the reign of Parakkamabāhu VI, in praise of this very king, whose 'long and glorious reign covering over half a century was the brightest period in the national annals nearest to the advent of the Portuguese'.[2]

[1] Geiger, *op. cit.*, p. 94.
[2] Fernando, *op. cit.*, Introduction, p. xviii.

Chapter II

LITERARY POSITION

The history of the *Vaṃsa* literature is fairly old in India. The word *vaṃsa* or *vaṃśa* itself was taken to mean *tanti* (lineage), which is just another word for *anvaya*. All the three words carry with them the idea of *paramparā* or lineal succession. Among the Brāhmaṇas, we have one bearing the title of *Vaṃśa-Brāhmaṇa*, which contains the lineal succession of the Brahman teachers of old. Such *vaṃśas* are appended to some of the chapters of the *Bṛhad Āraṇyaka Brāhmaṇa Upaniṣad*. So far as the Pali Canon is concerned, the *Buddhavaṃsa* is the only work which bears the *vaṃsa* title. Here, too, we have just a lineage of the greatest known teachers of mankind. The *Buddhavaṃsa*, which offers a traditional history of twenty-four Buddhas, including Gotama the historical Buddha, was supplemented later by the *Anāgatavaṃsa*, an ex-canonical work dealing with the legendary life of Metteyya the Future Buddha. Within the Pali Canon, the *Buddhavaṃsa* which is throughout a metrical composition of the chronicle type was preceded by a *Buddhāpadāna* (*Buddhāvadāna*) in the *Mahāpadāna Suttanta*. The *Buddhavaṃsa* itself has the *Apadāna* as companion work in verse. The *Buddhavaṃsa*, *Apadāna* and *Cariyā Piṭaka* are the three companion works which are to be counted among the latest additions to the *Khuddaka Nikāya*.

As between the Vaṃsa and the Apadāna which have narratives in common, we can do no more than drawing a broad distinction, premising that the main interest of the former lies in setting forth the lineage or succession, while the latter is primarily concerned with the edification of the tradition of meritorious and memorable deeds.

Corresponding to the lives of the Buddhas and those of the Theras in the *Buddhavaṃsa* and the *Apadāna* respectively, we have in the Jaina *Kalpa Sūtra* the lives of the Jinas or Tīrthaṅkaras and those of the disciples of Mahāvīra.

Both the *Vaṃsa Brāhmaṇa* and the *Vaṃśas* in the *Bṛhad Āraṇyaka Upaniṣad* are in prose. Whether prose had preceded verse or verse prose is still a disputed question. The alternation of prose and verse or of verse and prose is a phenomenon, which recurs even in the history of the *Vaṃsa* literature of Ceylon.

The earlier Indian prototypes of the *Vaṃsa* literature, mentioned above, are deficient in so far as they are wanting in the *rājavaṃsa* or *rājaparamparā*, while the *Vaṃsa* literature is mostly built on two *paramparās*, viz. *rāja* meaning the succession of kings and *thera* meaning the succession of elders.

The *rājavaṃsas* or *rājānvayas* were developing in India side by side with the *ācariyavaṃsa* or *ācariyaparamparās*. The origin of the former must be traced in the ancient *Itihāsas* or royal anecdotes, particularly in the pre-Pāṇinian *Mahābhārata*. The *rājavaṃsas* or dynastic lists came to form a distinctive feature as much of the Pauranic recast of the *Mahābhārata* as of the *Purāṇas* themselves. The traditions and lineages of kings in both prose and verse, are met with in the *Nikāyas* including the Canonical *Jātakas*. Out of these earlier prototypes emerged the *Vaṃsas* of Ceylon as a distinct and remarkable type of historical or semi-historical literature.

1. *Dīpavaṃsa*.—By the consensus of opinion this is the oldest known chronicle of Ceylon written in Pali. This text has been edited and translated by Oldenberg. This is, on the whole, a metrical composition with two prose passages, one of which is based upon a canonical text such as the Vinaya account of the Second Buddhist Council,[1] and the other is modelled evidently on the *Jātaka Nidāna-kathā*.[2] Whether these are later interpolations or remnants of the prose texts which were versified afterwards is still a disputed question. From the inclusion of the two prose passages within the present metrical form of the chronicle, no definite conclusion can be drawn either as to its original form or as to its literary position.

Arguing on the authority of the *Mahāvaṃsa Ṭīkā* which is the literary product of a much later age, Oldenberg inclines to the view that 'the author of the *Dīpavaṃsa* borrowed not only the materials of his own work, but also the mode of expression and even whole lines, word for word, from that *Aṭṭhakathā*' (Sinhalese *Aṭṭhakathā Mahāvaṃsa*).[3] The same

[1] *Dīpavaṃsa*, IV, bet. verses 46 and 47:

Tena kho pana samayena vassasatamhi parinibbute Bhagavati Vesālikā Vajjiputtakā bhikkhū Vesāliyaṃ dasa vatthūni dīpenti, etc.

Cf. *Vinaya Piṭaka*, II, p. 294.

[2] *Dīpavaṃsa*, XII, bet. verses 29 and 30:

Mārisa tvam pi Bhagavatā subyākato: anāgatamaddhāne Mahindo bhikkhu dīpam pasādayissati . . . Here the reminder, *Kālo mahāvīra dīpaṃ pasādetuṃ*, cannot but remind the reader of the stanza:

Kālo nu kho. . . . .

which occurs in the *Nidāna-kathā*, *Jātaka*, I, p. 48. Cf. *Paramatthadīpanī* on *Therīgāthā* (P.T.S.), p. 1.

[3] *Ibid.*, p. 6.

line of argument has been followed by Geiger, Malalasekera, and others who have seriously discussed the chronological and literary position of the *Dīpavaṃsa* in its present form. Apparently this is a very convincing argument, but on a closer examination it would seem that it moves in a vicious circle.

The Sinhalese *Aṭṭhakathā Mahāvaṃsa* is mentioned in the *Mahāvaṃsa Ṭīkā* as the basis of the *Mahāvaṃsa* proper written by the. Thera Mahānāma, a contemporary of Dhātusena and his son and successor, while in fact the *Mahāvaṃsa* was chiefly an improvement on the *Dīpavaṃsa* and its narrative was based upon a somewhat different traditional authority in places where it has differed from the *Dīpavaṃsa*. For this traditional authority Oldenberg has rightly drawn our attention to the *Aṭṭhakathā* version of the historical narrative of Mahinda's mission to Ceylon as found in the general introduction to the *Vinaya commentary*. But he is still guided or misguided by the author of the *Mahāvaṃsa Ṭīkā* when he observes: 'A considerable number of verses ascribed to the Porāṇā, i.e. taken from the ancient Sinhalese *Aṭṭhakathā* and quoted by Buddhaghosa or in the *Mahāvaṃsa Ṭīkā*, present the same close resemblance and almost identity with passages of the *Dīpavaṃsa*.' [1]

The fact is different. To Buddhaghosa, the celebrated Pali commentator, the *Dīpavaṃsa* was well known as a Pali chronicle. If the traditional verses quoted in the *Samantapāsādikā* in the name of the Porāṇā or ancient teachers be found to be identical with those in the *Dīpavaṃsa*, we are not to suppose that the prose account in the *Vinaya Aṭṭhakathā* with the verse-quotations inserted in it had formed the Sinhalese basis of the *Dīpavaṃsa* itself. The conclusion as to that would have been sound if it were the fact that the *Samantapāsādikā* account tallied entirely with the historical narrative of the *Dīpavaṃsa*. As already pointed out in the preceding chapter, the prose narrative in the *Samantapāsādikā* followed a somewhat different tradition in spite of the verse-quotations from the *Dīpavaṃsa*. Certain traditions recorded by the first-named Buddhaghosa are in accord with those in the *Dīpavaṃsa*; but these are missed in the narrative of the *Samantapāsādikā* and in the *Mahāvaṃsa* itself.[2]

When we say this, we do not mean to create the impression that the *Dīpavaṃsa* as a metrical composition had not for its

---

[1] *Dīpavaṃsa* (Oldenberg), Introduction, p. 5.

[2] Notably the prediction about the noble part to be played by Prince Piyadāsa (i.e. Piyadassana) on his becoming consecrated as king Asoka. *Sumaṅgala-vilāsinī*, II, p. 613.

basis any earlier legendary accounts in prose then available either in Pali or in Sinhalese. All that we mean to say is that the answer to the question regarding the literary position of the *Dīpavaṃsa* does not lie in the *Aṭṭhakathā Mahāvaṃsa* as made out from the *Samantapāsādikā* and the *Mahāvaṃsa Ṭīkā*; it lies elsewhere.

The *Buddhavaṃsa* offers us the Pali canonical model for the metrical form of the *Dīpavaṃsa.* Both the works are composed in an *Anuṣṭubh* metre and in a simple narrative style. The variation in metre is seldom noticed. Anything approaching real poetry in the *Buddhavaṃsa* is to be noticed in its introductory verses and *Sumedha-kathā*, and anything approaching real poetry in the *Dīpavaṃsa* lies in its introductory verses and a few verses which are composed in a different metre in its first two chapters.

Buddhavaṃsa:

Obhāsitā ca paṭhavī sadevakā
puthū ca lokantarikā asaṃvutā ।
tamo ca tibbo vihato tadā ahu
disvāna accherakaṃ pāṭihīraṃ ॥
Sadevagandhabbamanussarakkhase
ābhā uḷārā vipulā ajāyatha ।
imasmiṃ loke parasmiṃ cobhayasmiṃ
adho ca uddhaṃ tiriyañ ca vitthataṃ ॥

Dīpavaṃsa:

Suṇātha sabbe paṇidhāya mānasaṃ,
vaṃsaṃ pavakkhāmi paramparāgataṃ ।
thutippasatthaṃ bahunābhivaṇṇitaṃ
etaṃhi nānākusumaṃ va ganthitaṃ ॥
Anūpamaṃ vaṃsavaraggavāsīnaṃ
apubbaṃ anaññaṃ tatha suppakāsitaṃ ।
ariyāgataṃ uttamasabbhi vaṇṇitaṃ
suṇātha dīpatthuti sādhusakkataṃ ॥

Also:

Rammaṃ manuññaṃ haritaṃ susītalaṃ
ārāmavanarāmaṇeyyakaṃ varaṃ ।
santīdha phullaphaladhārino dumā,
suññaṃ vivittaṃ, na ca koci issaro ॥
mahaṇṇave sāgaravārimajjhe sugambhīre
ūmi sadā pabhijjare, ।
suduggame pabbatajālamussite
sudukkaraṃ attha anitthamantaraṃ ॥

Here, in the stanzas cited above, is a conscious effort made towards producing the effect of *kāvya* poetry. Their composer had before him the canonical model in some of the Psalms of the Early Buddhist Brothers and Sisters in the *Thera-Therī-gāthā*. These, as they stand in the first two chapters of the *Dīpavaṃsa*, serve to relieve the monotony and dulness of the purely historical narrative of the chronicle. Had such stanzas been introduced also in the remaining chapters, the chronicle might have assumed the form of a *kāvya*. As regards some of the remaining chapters, the compiler has sought to break the monotony of the metrical narration of historical events by introducing certain statements in prose. So far as the narrations in the colourless *Anuṣṭubh* metre are concerned, they were modelled evidently on the traditional sayings in verse then current in the community indefinitely in the name of the *Porāṇas* or Ancient Teachers.

With Geiger the *Dīpavaṃsa* represents the first unaided struggle to create an epic out of already existing material.[1] He is inclined also to think that the *Dīpavaṃsa* closely resembles in form the ancient *Ākhyāna* poetry of India, the characteristic feature of which lies in this that the entire story is not yet established in a form, but only certain parts are metrically fixed and thereby are secured from further departure from the tradition. This chronicle was evidently the production of an age when with the decline of oral tradition, the same stories came to show many variants, together with many examples of identity of language.[2]

The question still remains—can the *Dīpavaṃsa* in its present form be judged at all as an epic? To be an epic, it must have a narrative interweaving several episodes into a unity, showing the dramatic junctures and conveying a central idea or moral; its theme, too, must be lofty and of heroic character, and above all, there must be a hero whose exploits it must narrate in an effective manner.

So far as the narrative of the *Dīpavaṃsa* is concerned, the historical motive predominates over the poetical. The heroes, too, are not one but many. Its main theme is *Laṅkā-vijaya*, the conquest of Laṅkā, both culturally and politically, first, by the Buddha, secondly, by prince Vijaya, and thirdly, by the Thera Mahinda. King Devānampiya Tissa and Duṭṭhagāmaṇi were the two great national heroes of Ceylon who served to consolidate the territory conquered for the

---

[1] Geiger, *The Dīpavaṃsa and Mahāvaṃsa*, p. 2.

[2] *Ibid.*, p. 11.

religion of Sākyamuni. Viewed in this light, the narrative of the *Dīpavaṃsa* is a combination of as many as five epics. The *Mahāvaṃsa* closes each of its chapters with the pathetic reflection setting forth the evanescent character of the kingly career and dynastic rule and emphasizing the value of the meritorious deeds that only endure.[1] This kind of reflection constituting the central idea or moral of the *Mahāvaṃsa* is met with once at the end of the *Mahārājavaṃsa* section of the *Dīpavaṃsa* forming the epic kernel, and next at the end of the concluding chapter:

> *Aniccā vata saṃkhārā uppādavayadhammino* ।
> *uppajjitvā nirujjhanti, tesaṃ vūpasamo sukho* ॥ [2]
>
> *Asādhusaṃgamen'eva yāvajīvaṃ subhāsubhaṃ* ।
> *katvā gato yathākammaṃ so Mahāsenabhūpati* ॥
> *Tasmā asādhusaṃsaggaṃ ārakā parivajjiya* ।
> *ahiṃ vāsīvisaṃ vāsi kareyy'atthahitaṃ bhave* ॥ [3]

It will be seen that the moral at the end of the *Mahārāja-vaṃsa* section is not an original composition but a stanza taken over from the *Mahāparinibbāna Suttanta*, Chapter VI, and that at the end of Chapter XXII, too, it is just an adaptation to the traditional moral met with in the *Jātakas*.

The main drawbacks of the earlier Pali chronicle as regards its mode of narration of events lie, as pointed out by the author of the *Mahāvaṃsa*, in the fact that it is in some places too diffusive and in some places too concise, and what is more, it abounds in repetitions.

Judged from the point of view of poetry, its main defect, as suggested in the opening verses of the *Mahāvaṃsa*, consists in its failure to kindle faith and to call up emotion in right places (*pasādajanake ṭhāne tathā saṃvegakārake*).

These points of criticism should, however, be considered, first of all, with reference to the earlier form of the *Dīpavaṃsa* in which its principal themes were Buddha's visits to Ceylon, the conquest of the island by Prince Vijaya, the origin of the Buddhist sects and schools of thought, and the establishment of the Buddhist Orders by Mahinda and Saṅghamittā.

So far as this earlier form of the chronicle is concerned, its author openly claims that his performance is capable of awakening emotional interest, pleasing and delighting the

[1] Cf. Barua, *Ceylon Lectures*, p. 280.
[2] *Dīpavaṃsa*, III, 50.
[3] *Ibid.*, XXII, 75-76.

heart of the reader, and what is more, the narrative of his epic is replete with various forms and modes:

> *pīti-pāmojja-janana*ṃ *pasādeyya*ṃ *manorama*ṃ
> *anekākārasampanna*ṃ.......................

That there is lack of symmetry here and there is undeniable. The events are not narrated in one and the same strain. The result produced is, on the whole, a piece of mosaic. But therein exactly lies its rugged beauty and grandeur. The repetitions complained of are there, but that is more apparent than real. Let us take, for instance, the account of the First Buddhist Council which occurs twice in the *Dīpavaṃsa*, first, in Chapter IV and, again, in Chapter V. On looking more closely into the matter, however, we find that in the first instance the author is to offer us a description of the Council concerned as an isolated incident, considered *per se*, and in the second context it is presented as an integral part of the whole of the historical narrative. The same as to the description of the Second Buddhist Council. The so-called repetitions are not unjustified.

The narration of events from the reign of the immediate successor of Devānaṃpiya Tissa to that of Mahāsena is dominated by purely historical motive. The strain of continuous narration is nowhere sought to be relieved. The thread of the narrative is loose and the accounts in places are too concise to produce a lasting effect. It is not unlikely that the four or five concluding chapters were later additions.

2. *Aṭṭhakathā Mahāvaṃsa*.—The Sinhalese original of this work being irrevocably lost, its literary position depends on its Pali versions in the commentaries attributed to Buddhaghosa, notably, the *Sumaṅgalavilāsinī*, the *Atthasālinī*, the *Kathāvatthu-aṭṭhakathā* and the *Samantapāsādikā*. The historical matters are mostly to be found in the general introduction and rarely in the body of the commentaries. The accounts are in prose interspersed with traditional verses cited either from the *Dīpavaṃsa* or current in the name of the ancient teachers (*Porāṇā*). Strangely enough, the verses traceable in the *Dīpavaṃsa* are attributed to the *Porāṇas* in the *Mahāvaṃsa Ṭīkā*, while the verse-quotations from the *Porāṇas* which are met with in the Pali canonical commentaries stand altogether on a different footing, and so far as their style of composition is concerned, they represent a stage of literary development anterior to that of the *Dīpavaṃsa*.

The general introduction to the *Kathāvatthu-aṭṭhakathā* goes to show that the statement in prose is based upon the metrical account cited *in extenso* from the *Dīpavaṃsa*. The description of the First Buddhist Council given by Buddhaghosa in the general introduction to his *Sumaṅgalavilāsinī* is based partly on the Vinaya account in the *Cullavagga*, Chapter XI, and partly on a later tradition. Here the prose style of Buddhaghosa is laboured, heavy and pedantic. The case is somewhat different when we read the general introduction to the *Vinaya Aṭṭhakathā* where the author writes with comparative ease and his mode of presentation of the subject is characterized by lucidity and spontaneity. Here the prose style is well suited to a purely historical narrative. The Legends of Asoka, as narrated in the *Divyāvadāna*, show a conscious effort for producing a poetical effect.

3. *Mahāvaṃsa.*—This work certainly stands as a masterpiece produced by the poetically gifted Thera Mahānāma in the *Vaṃsa* literature of Ceylon. It is undoubtedly the more finished product of the literary and poetical art employed in the earlier works of the same type, particularly in the *Dīpavaṃsa.* It is not unreasonably judged as the national epic of Ceylon with Duṭṭhagāmaṇi as its chief hero. Kalhaṇa's *Rājataraṅgiṇī* and the anonymous *Mūlakalpa* are two later Sanskrit chronicles in verse which are without the epic touch of the *Mahāvaṃsa.* Firdausi's *Shāhnāmāh*, which occupies a high place in the world of epics, is a similar chronicle of the ancient kings of Iran. Just as Firdausi's masterpiece was in one sense the completed form of the chronicle left unfinished by Dāqiqi, so in another sense Mahānāma's masterpiece may be regarded as the developed form of the *Dīpavaṃsa* as regards its four or five concluding chapters. Malalasekera says, 'Mahānāma was no genius, he was too much hide-bound by tradition, and his work cannot rank as a literary performance of the first order.'[1] But it is contended that it may not be an epic of as high literary merit as Vālmīki's *Rāmāyaṇa*, Sauti's *Mahābhārata* or Firdausi's *Shāhnāmāh.* It is an epic throughout with a keen sense of history, the simplicity of diction, the purity of style and the sobriety of judgement. Its central idea or moral looms large at the end of each chapter. The national mind, self-consciousness and character have found a permanent expression in it.[2]

In claiming the superiority of artistic workmanship in his treatment of one and the same theme, the author of the *Mahāvaṃsa* was compelled to point out the drawbacks in the earlier chronicle. Repetitions, diffuseness and unmethodical representation are the three main faults in the earlier work

---

[1] *Pali Literature of Ceylon*, p. 141.

[2] *Ceylon Lectures*, p. 100.

which he consciously sought to avoid in his own composition and presentation. While commenting on this literary position of Mahānāma's work, Geiger rightly observes: 'The *Mahāvaṃsa* compared with the *Dīpavaṃsa* has every claim to be regarded as a work of art. The story proceeds in it in a logical manner, without inconvenient breaks or repetitions. It runs parallel with the *Dīpavaṃsa* at times in such a way that whole episodes in both epics are evidently two different versifications of the same material. But the *Mahāvaṃsa* amplifies and supplements the *Dīpavaṃsa*, or else represents the subject in a more concise manner. The greater ability is shown in the handling of speech and metre in the *Mahāvaṃsa* in contrast to the *Dīpavaṃsa* . . . Also the niceties of diction, especially the play upon words, is more evident in the *Mahāvaṃsa* than in the *Dīpavaṃsa*. To sum up, we notice everywhere in the *Mahāvaṃsa* the hand of a poet, working deliberately, lingering over his material, and endeavouring to clothe it in suitable form.'[1]

Notwithstanding this fact, looking more closely into the matter, one cannot help saying that the whole foundation of the great national epic of Ceylon was laid in the earlier chronicle. The *Dīpavaṃsa* adopted, as we saw, its own literary and poetical devices. It had different heroes in the successive stages of its narrative, while the *Mahāvaṃsa* came to shift its emphasis and lay it on Duṭṭhagāmaṇi. The diction of the *Mahāvaṃsa* was modelled evidently on the concluding chapters of the *Dīpavaṃsa*. The *Mahāvaṃsa* would have been a poem written in high strain and its effect would have been monotonous and tiresome but for the fact its author broke the monotony and relieved the tension by his indulgence in reflective poetry at the end of each chapter, and wisdom in effecting a change in metre.

4. *Extended Mahāvaṃsa*.—The extended *Mahāvaṃsa* is nothing but a later enlarged version or recension of the poem of Mahānāma. This text has been edited by G. P. Malalasekera in the *Aluvihāra series*, Vol. III, and published by the Royal Asiatic Society (Ceylon Branch), 1937. Curiously enough, the work is represented in the colophon as one consisting of thirty-five *bhāṇavāras* or chapters, while the work in its present form contains thirty-seven chapters.

Imāya pañcatiṃsamattāya bhāṇavārāya ganthato
yam etaṃ niṭṭhapentena puññaṃ upacitaṃ mayā

(Colophon).

[1] *Dīpavaṃsa and Mahāvaṃsa*, p. 17.

Moggallāna introduces himself as the author of this work. But apart from the fact that for additional matter the author was indebted to the *Buddhavaṃsa*, *Līnattha* and *Thūpavaṃsa*, the literary position of the work is the same as that of Mahānāma's epic upon which it was based. The reflective stanzas at the end of the chapters are identical in both the versions.

5. *Cūḷavaṃsa.*—If the extended *Mahāvaṃsa* is an enlarged version of the *Mahāvaṃsa* written by Mahānāma, the *Cūḷavaṃsa* certainly represents a later continuation of the same. In other words, the *Cūḷavaṃsa* is just a supplement to the *Mahāvaṃsa*. Though it grew up into its present form through two or three stages, the poet of each stage was careful to maintain the diction and style of Mahānāma. The epic character of the work is sought to be maintained by means of the reflective stanzas with which each chapter is concluded. In going to convey the moral in the concluding stanza of Chapter 100, the later poet appears to have exceeded the limits of reflective poetry by his naive indulgence in an admonition:

Bhoge ca dehe ca asārakattaṃ
mantvālayaṃ dūrataraṃ haranti
tumhe pi vatthuttayam eva seviya
lokuttarādiṃ kusalaṃ bhajavho.

6. *Vaṃsatthappakāsinī.*[1]—This is the later convenient name applied to the Pali commentary on the *Mahāvaṃsa alias Padyapadoruvaṃsa* written by the Thera Mahānāma II and known by the name of *Padyapadoruvaṃsavaṇṇanā* and *Vaṃsatthappakāsinī*. In the author's own description the work was not a mere translation from any earlier Sinhalese *Aṭṭhakathā*; it was rather a digest (*atthasāraṃ*) of earlier works carefully prepared in the diction of the Pali Canon (*tantinayānurūpena*). The main earlier works utilized by him consisted of (1) the text of the *Mahāvaṃsa* in its two recensions, (2) the *Aṭṭhakathā Mahāvaṃsa*, (3) two Sinhalese commentaries on the *Mahāvaṃsa*, *viz.* those belonging to the Mahāvihāra and Abhayagiri fraternities, (4) the *Samantapāsādikā*, (5) the *Dīpavaṃsa Aṭṭhakathā*, (6) the *Jātaka Nidāna-kathā*, (7) the *Sahassavatthu-aṭṭhakathā*, (8) the *Mahābodhivaṃsa-aṭṭhakathā*, (9) the *Ganṭhipadatthavaṇṇanā*, and (10) the *Sīhalanamakkāra-vaṇṇanā*.

The prose style of the commentary is simple and lucid; it is hardly involved or ornate. There are only two or three

[1] Edited for the Government of Ceylon by G. P. Malalasekera in two volumes and published by the P.T.S., London (1935).

ornamental passages, as pointed out by Malalasekera, who particularly draws our attention to the description of the Mahāmeghavana (72, 11ff.) and the passage on the scenic beauties of Ceylon (321, 3ff.).[1] It appears that the graphic description of Ceylon is modelled on the Milinda description of the Yona city of Sāgala and partly also on Buddhadatta's description of the port of Kāveripaṭṭana: *tattha tattha sannivesita - gāmanigama - nagara - janapada - rājadhānī - vāpi - taḷākapokkharaṇī - uyyānabhūmippadesehi - pavaraṅgapaccaṅga - rūpissariya - samannāgatāya sampannasalilāsayasaṃvaḍ - ḍhapupphaphalapallava - vicittataruvanagahana - racita* . . .[2]

The following two stanzas composed by the author distinctly betray the influence of later artificial *kāvya* poetry:

Budhajanapadumaravibhūtanuttaro
Vararavikulambarapabhāsituttamo
Saddhammakiraṇakaravaratejasā yo
Mohandhakārahananamhi mahānubhāvo.[3]

7. *Mahābodhivaṃsa.*—The *Mahābodhivaṃsa*[4] has been written with freedom and prolixity common to Buddhist writers. The author of this work has borrowed largely from the sources as well as from the *Mahāvaṃsa* text. There is enough evidence to show that the author has made use of other materials as well. The chapters relating to the three Councils and the rehearsal of the Law are similar not only to the Buddhist account in the introduction to the *Sumaṅgalavilāsinī* but also to that in the *Saddhammasaṅgaha*. As regards the description of Mahinda's adventures after his arrival in Laṅkā, the *Mahābodhivaṃsa* and the *Samantapāsādikā* are in agreement.

The Pali text of the *Mahābodhivaṃsa* is a translation of a Sinhalese original. It tells us nothing about its author. According to the *Sāsanavaṃsadīpa*, Upatissa was its author.

Upatissamahāthero Māgadhāya niruttiyā
Bodhivamsaṃ akā dhīro dhīrehi abhivaṇṇiyam.

The *Gandhavaṃsa* points out that the *Mahābodhivaṃsa* was written independently by its author. The style is easy and the language is lucid.

---

[1] *Vaṃsatthappakāsinī*, Introd., p. cvii.

[2] Cf. *Milinda*, pp. 1-2: *Atthi Yonakānam nānāpuṭabhedanam Sāgalaṃ nāma nagaraṃ nadīpabbata sobhitam ramaṇīyabhūmipadesabhāgaṃ ārāmuyyānopavana taḷākapokkharaṇī sampannaṃ nadīpabbatavanarāmaṇeyyakaṃ* . . .
Also Buddhadatta's *Manuals* edited by A. P. Buddhadatta, 1915, preface, p. xiii.

[3] *Vaṃsatthappakāsinī*, I, p. 1.

[4] This text has been edited by S. Arthur Strong for the P.T.S. (1891).

8. *Thūpavaṃsa.*—In the introductory verses the author tells us that the work having at first been compiled in Sinhalese language was not accessible to all. Even the earlier Māgadhī (i.e. Pali) version perpared for the benefit of all was full of defective arrangement and language and it left out many things that ought to have been narrated. In order to remove these defects in the earlier Māgadhī version the author undertook to do the work again.

Vākyena Sīhala-bhāvena 'bhisaṅkhatattā |
atthaṃ na sādhayati sabbajanassa sammā ||
Yasmā ca Māgadha-niruttikato 'pi Thūpa- |
vaṃso viruddha-naya-sadda-samākulo so ||
vattabban eva ca bahuṃ pi yato na vuttaṃ |
tasmā ahaṃ punapi vaṃsaṃ imaṃ vadāmi ||

Though the earlier Pali text is no longer extant, it is not difficult to estimate the nature of the linguistic improvement effected by Vācissara by comparing his version of the *Thūpavaṃsa* with parallel passages as found in the *Samantapāsādikā* or the *Sumaṅgalavilāsinī*.

I. (*a*) *Devānampiyatisso mahārājā 'pi kho Sumanasāmaṇerassa vacanena māgasiramāsassa paṭhamapāṭipadadivasato pabhuti uttaradvārato paṭṭhāya yāva Jambukolapaṭṭanaṃ maggaṃ sodhāpetvā alaṃkārāpetvā nagarato nikkhamana-divase.*[1]

(*b*) *Devānampiyatissa-mahārājā 'pi uttaradvārato paṭṭhāya yāva Jambukolapaṭṭanā maggaṃ sodhāpetvā alaṅkārāpetvā nagarato nikkhamana-divase.*[2]

II. (*a*) *Tena ca samayena rājadhītā Saṃghamittā 'pi tasmiṃ yeva ṭhāneṭhitā hoti tassā ca sāmiko Aggibrahmā nāma kumāro . . . Rājā taṃ disvā āha.*[3]

(*b*) *Tena ca samayena rājadhītā Saṅghamittā 'pi tasmiṃ ṭhāneṭhitā hoti, taṃ disvā āha.*[4]

The only interesting point to be noticed in the whole work is the setting out of legendary materials having their bearings upon the history of the *Thūpas.* The *Thūpavaṃsa* undoubtedly is one of the products of the decadent period of Pali literature in Ceylon. It is lacking in originality and the atmosphere of life it creates is dull and monotonous. It is a specimen of the stereotyped and highly conventionalized prose of scholastic writings.

9. *Dāṭhāvaṃsa.*—The *Dāṭhāvaṃsa* is a quasi-religious historical record written with the intention of edifying (*pasādasaṃvegakara*) or rousing (somebody's) religious emo-

---

[1] *Samantapāsādikā*, I, p. 98.
[2] *Thūpavaṃsa*, p. 53.
[3] *Samantapāsādikā*, I, p. 51.
[4] *Thūpavaṃsa*, p. 42.

tions. It bears many marks of the fairy tale. It is remarkable because it shows us Pali as a medium of epic poetry. In it the character of classical Pali is well retained, although the Sanskrit education of its author has left its stamp on its style. We find the old vocabulary enriched by adapted Sanskrit words; single expressions are turned into long compounds[1] after the fashion of the Sanskrit *kāvya* literature. Such words as *antarāla, avadāta, āmoda, nikhila, nūtana, dhavala,* occur in large numbers. Some metaphorical expressions are also found there. It is an excellent piece of poetry. Its vocabulary is rich. In the first chapter the verses are written in *Jagatī* metre, sixty stanzas in *Vaṃśastha,* and the last two in *Sragdharā.* The second chapter is composed of verses in *Anuṣṭubh, Pathyavaktra* and *Mandākrāntā.* The third chapter has verses composed of *Triṣṭubh, Upajāti, Indravajrā, Upendra-vajrā* and *Śikhariṇī.* The fourth chapter contains verses in *Atiśarkarī* and *Śārdūlavikrīḍita.* The last chapter employs *Śarkarī, Vasantatilakā* and *Sragdharā* metres.

10. *Saddhammasaṅgaha.*—The *Saddhammasaṅgaha*[2] is written in an elegant and simple language. It belongs to the class of manuals and as such it is a mixture of prose and poetry. In most cases the prose portion serves only as an explanation of the subject matter in verse. This work contains many discourses common to the *Mahābodhivaṃsa,* the *Gandhavaṃsa,* the *Sāsanavaṃsa* and the like. The author has borrowed very largely from the actual texts of the *Dīpavaṃsa,* the *Mahāvaṃsa,* the *Aṭṭhakathā* and other well-known Pali works which are simply referred to as *Porāṇā* or ancient authorities. The author refers to many works among which some may be noted here: *Sāratthadīpanī* or the *Atthavaṇṇanā* of the *Samantapāsādikā,* the *Vinaya Commentary;* the *Atthavaṇṇanā* of the *Sumaṅgalavilāsinī,* the *Dīgha Nikāya Commentary;* the *Atthavaṇṇanā* of the *Papañcasūdanī,* the *Majjhima Nikāya Commentary;* the *Atthavaṇṇanā* of the *Sāratthappakāsinī,* the *Saṃyutta Nikāya Commentary;* the *Atthavaṇṇanā* of the *Manorathapūraṇī,* the *Aṅguttara Nikāya Commentary,* and the *Atthavaṇṇanā* of the *Atthasālinī,* the *Dhammasaṅgaṇi Commentary.*

11. *Later Sinhalese Chronicles.*—They are either translations or prose amplifications of the Pali books. They cannot be taken to represent the older Sinhalese works presupposed

[1] *E.g.*, IV, 46.

[2] This text has been edited by N. Saddhānanda for *J.P.T.S.*, 1890, and translated into English by B. C. Law entitled '*A Manual of Buddhist Historical Traditions*', published by the University of Calcutta (1941).

by the Pali compilations. The prose style of the Sinhalese *Dhātuvaṃsa* was determined entirely by its Pali original, the *Nalāṭa Dhātuvaṃsa*. Occasional differences in style, as noticed in the *Rājāvalī*, are evidently due to the fact that 'the author has taken many passages word for word from older sources'. Those who are better acquainted with the Sinhalese language and literature are competent to judge their style of composition. These later Sinhalese chronicles appear to us as literary productions of a dull and decadent age.

Chapter III

HISTORICAL POSITION

The chronicles of Ceylon were all written or compiled by the Elders whose primary interest naturally lay in the history of Buddhism and Buddhist foundations. Although the religious motive finding its expression in the edification of all things connected with Buddhism, predominates over everything else, there is really an interplay throughout of two distinct motives, devotional and patriotic. The first of them may be construed as puritanic and sectarian, and the second as national and racial. Just as the religious motive cannot be divorced from the cultural advancement, so the patriotic motive cannot be separated from the promotion of the general cause of piety. The belief in miracle and supernaturalism has had its due rôle. Proper allowance must have to be made also for the inventive power of imagination behind some of the legends that have found their place in sober historical narratives. But, in spite of all these, it is now admitted on all hands that the chronicles of Ceylon are not full of mendacious fictions, their kernel and main bulk being history, nothing but history. The modern idea of sober and authentic history may be absent, but their permanent value as an indispensable source-book of history remains unchallenged. In fact in the absence of inscriptions, archaeological finds and foreign accounts, the chronicles only deal with the early history of Ceylon. The later history of Ceylon from Kittisiri-Meghavaṇṇa stands on a solid basis of fact as presented in the *Cūḷavaṃsa*, and does not, therefore, need much comment. The historical position of the chronicles needs clarification in so far as they are concerned with the early history of the island and it may be worth while to examine it, period by period.

1. *Pre-historic period.*—The chronicles speak of a prehistoric period during which the island of Ceylon had undergone changes in its names before it came to be known by the name of Laṅkādīpa or Tambapaṇṇidīpa. These periods are conceived in terms of the successive dispensations of the four Buddhas, Kakusandha, Koṇāgamana, Kassapa, and Gotama, the advent of all of whom took place in the present era or æon of cosmic evolution, the development of the earth as the abode of men. The island which was known by the name of Ojadīpa in Kakusandha's time became known by the name of

Varadīpa during the next dispensation. It was called Maṇḍadīpa in the time of Kassapa, and Laṅkādīpa and Tambapaṇṇidīpa in Gotama's time.

The island had different capitals in succession: Abhayapura, Vaḍḍhamāna, Visāla, and Anurādhapura. Four different mountains came into prominence: Devakūṭa, Sumanakūṭa, Subhakūṭa, and Cetiyapabbata. Evidently the Buddhist chroniclers built up these legends on the basis of the Indian legends of the Buddhas in such canonical texts as the *Mahāpadāna Suttanta* and the *Buddhavaṃsa*. However pious may be their motive, these cannot but appear to modern students as incredible and unhistorical. They will certainly be reluctant to go so far as to believe in miracles and supernormal powers upon which depends the credibility of visits and preachings by which the four great Buddhas of the present era sanctified the island in the pre-historic period of its history and culture. The chronicles are far from giving us a realistic account of the remains of the handicrafts of men who lived in the Palæolithic and Neolithic Ages. But they introduce us surely to two powerful aboriginal races of Yakkhas and Nāgas who held sway over the island previous to the establishment of the Aryan rule. They are unaware of the Veddās who are taken to be present descendants of the Palæolithic dwellers. They have nothing to say about the Śabaras whose name lingers in the name of the village called Habaragāma. They make mention, on the other hand, of the Pulindas as a mixed race of aborigines who sprang from the union of an Indian prince with a Yakkhinī. The Yakkhas, and Nāgas, too, appear at first sight as semi-mythical and semi-human savages who deserved to be tamed, defeated and destroyed. That there previously existed an island known by a certain name with its noted mountain-peaks and hills is undeniable. But as regards its primitive inhabitants, the chronicles speak very lightly of them, and the accounts they give of them are at variance in some important respects with those met with elsewhere.[1]

The invention of pious legends regarding the inestimable favour done to the country and its inhabitants by the Buddha through his miraculous visits and acts of grace was not peculiar to the chronicles of Ceylon. There were similar legends invented and cherished in other countries where Buddhism became the living faith of the people. But the Ceylon chroniclers far excelled others in this art.

---

[1] *Valāhassa Jātaka*, No. 196, *Jataka*, II, pp. 127–130; its Sanskrit version in the *Divyāvadāna*, pp. 523ff.; Beal, *Buddhist Records of the Western World*, I, p. lxxii; Beal, *op. cit.*, II, pp. 239ff.; McCrindle, *Ancient India*, pp. 60ff., 173ff.

The taming of the Yakkhas and Nāgas by the historical Buddha was in no way new. The Sutta and Vinaya Piṭakas record many instances thereof. The novelty lay only in the skilful adaptation of the canonical examples to different local conditions with all the ingenuity and the air of plausibility and truth. The lead given in the *Dīpavaṃsa* was faithfully followed in the later chronicles without any questioning about its reasonableness or soundness. It is interesting nevertheless to consider the historical information which can be gathered from the legendary accounts.

A. It is claimed that the plains of Laṅkā or Tambapaṇṇi were inhabited by men in the old ages, even when it was known as Ojadīpa, Varadīpa or Maṇḍadīpa. At the time of the rise of Buddhism the land was covered with great forests and full of horrors. It came then to be inhabited by the Yakkhas and such savage kinsmen as the Rākkhasas and Pisācas who were of various shapes and hideous forms, full of fury and wrath, wicked backbiters, pitiless and cruel, violent and merciless, and harmful. Thus the island stood badly in need of being secured against them, so that it might again be the peaceful, delightful, and congenial habitat of a large number of men.

B. The first wise and effective step to be taken was to follow the doctrine of segregation, the island of Laṅkā being reserved for the higher races of men and Giridīpa allotted to the predatory savages. The second island stood in close proximity to the first, and in their physical features they were almost alike; the latter was in some respects even superior to the former. Here the description of the two islands seems to be vivid and accurate. They had high and low lands, beautifully adorned with rivers, mountains and lakes, free from danger, well protected, surrounded by the ocean, rich in food-grains and blessed with a well-tempered climate. They were charming and delightful, green and cool, adorned with gardens and forests, fruit and flower trees, provided with ample living spaces, and subject to no master.

C. Geiger identifies Giridīpa with the highlands in the interior of Ceylon on the twofold ground: (1) that the word *dīpa* was formerly used in a wider sense, and (2) that the Yakkhas (evidently meaning the Veddās) are still to be found in Ceylon in later times.[1] This is not at all convincing, since the highlands in the interior of Ceylon are not separated from the mainland, and are not surrounded by the ocean.

[1] *Mahāvaṃsa*, Geiger's translation, p. 4.

D. In the next stage we find that within a few years the island of Laṅkā became a scene of conflict between the Nāgas who are distinguished as those who were dwellers of the sea, the dwellers of the mountains, and those of a riverine region at the mouth of the river Kalyāṇī. They are represented as matrimonially connected, while their kings are called *Mahodara* (big-bellied), *Cūḷodara* (small bellied), and *Maṇi-akkhika* (gem-eyed). The name of Nāgadīpa apparently forming a part of Ceylon was derived from the Nāga settlers. The chroniclers were probably guilty of a confusion made between Nāga meaning serpents and Nāga standing for nagga (naked ones).

E. In the third stage at about the time of the Buddha's demise the chronicles go to depict a scene in which Ceylon is divided into two Yakkha principalities, the western one with Sirīsavatthu as its main city and the eastern one having Laṅkā for its capital. Strangely enough, Sirīsavatthu, which is mentioned in the Pali Valāhassa Jātaka, as the prosperous port and main city of Tambapaṇṇi division of Ceylon, is described here as the capital of the western Yakkha principality, situated below Tambapaṇṇidīpa.

F. In these connections the chronicles draw our attention to the sanctified site of the Subhaṅgaṇa Thūpa on the bank of a river near Mahiya Pokkhala, to Guidīpa (modern Karadivo), the riverine region of Kalyāṇī (Kaelani), the principal river of Ceylon which flows down into the sea to the north of Colombo, the sites of the Kalyāṇī-cetiya, the Dīghavāpi-cetiya, Meghavanārāma, Mahābodhi-cetiya, Mahāthūpa, Thūpārāma-cetiya, Mahiyaṅgana-thūpa, and Mahānāga garden on the bank of the river called Gaṅgā or Mahāgaṅgā (modern Mahāwaeligaṅgā).

As a fitting introduction to the historical drama of Buddhism in Ceylon it is not enough to impress the reader with the high antiquity and sanctity of the island forming the scene of action. The Mahārājavaṃsa or great line of illustrious rulers in whose family Gotama the Buddha, the main actor and hero, was born, is indispensable as a means of heightening its antiquity and importance. Gotama's descent is traced from Mahāsammata, the first elected ruler and leader of men through three stages: from Mahāsammata to Accimā, from Accimā to Nemiya, and from Nemiya to Suddhodana, father of Siddhārtha-Gotama—a theological device followed in the Gospels of Jesus Christ.[1] The family-

[1] St. Matthew, I. 17: 'So all the generations from Abraham to David are

line may be briefly traced from king Okkāka (Ikṣvāku), the pride being taken in having Gotama as a scion of the Solar race of Khattiyas. The illustrious predecessors of Jesus of Nazareth were all great patriarchs and prophets born in the Hebrew race, and their noble traditions are embodied in the Old Testament. As regards the illustrious predecessors of Gotama of Kapilavatthu, many of them are passing shadows, mere names, and the traditions of a few only are still preserved in the Jātakas and other Indian works. The chroniclers of Ceylon were not bound to vouchsafe for the authenticity of the long string of ornamental names.[1]

2. *Beginning of historical period.*—The sequence of events which is the essence of historical narratives needs a framework of chronology. This is sought to be built in the chronicles of Ceylon on a twofold succession, the succession of rulers and ruling dynasties (*rāja-paramparā*) and the succession of the leading Elders (*thera-paramparā*).[2] The comparative continuity of the first being greater, the chronicles naturally rely more upon it. The chronology must begin from a certain definite date, which, in the case of the Ceylon chronicles, is the year of the Buddha's demise, making the starting point of the Buddha Era (*Buddhavassa*).

A happy coincidence is imagined and availed of to build up a systematic chronology of the kings of Ceylon, the coincidence of the day of the Buddha's demise with that of the landing of the exiled prince Vijaya on the island of Laṅkā.[3] A prediction is put into the mouth of the Buddha to raise the importance of his appearance on the island as the founder of the first Aryan rule. An account is given of the circumstances that led to the banishment of the prince which proved to be a blessing in disguise for the future history of the island as a whole.

The chroniclers who were mad with the idea of the Indo-Aryan rule did not foresee the difficulties to be met by the modern historian. The abruptness of the establishment of an Indian form of monarchy goes against other historical traditions that sensibly represent it as the final result of an earlier and long process of settlement and colonization. They are silent altogether on the previous trade-connection of the island with the mainland of India. They are unaware of the tradition narrating how a leader of sea-going Indian merchants

---

fourteen generations; and from the carrying away into Babylon unto Christ are fourteen generations.'

[1] *Dīpavaṃsa*, III; *Mahāvaṃsa*, II; Geiger's translation, pp. 10ff.

[2] Rhys Davids, *Buddhist Suttas* (*S.B.E.*, Vol. XI), Intro., pp. xlvi ff.

[3] *Dīpavaṃsa*, IX, 21; *Mahāvaṃsa*, VII, 1–3.

figured ultimately as the first monarch of Ceylon and the founder of the first ruling dynasty. Neither the process of colonization nor that of linguistic development could have taken place so soon. They would have us believe that the conqueror of the island then under the sway of the Yakkhas, and the founder of the first monarchy favourable to the propagation of Buddhism, was the banished crown prince Vijaya, the son of king Sīhabāhu of the country of Lāḷa, with Sīhapura as its capital, and the grandson of the king of Vaṅga on his maternal side. The location suggested leaves no room for doubt that the chroniclers kept in view Rāḍha (Ardhamāgadhī Lāḍha) meaning West Bengal and Siṃhapura on the northern border of the country of Kaliṅga. The legend[1] recorded by Hiuen Tsang mentions South India as the scene of action of the lion and the princess. Presumably behind this legend was the history of Siṃhapura on the southern portion of Kaliṅga. The fondness of the people of Ceylon for the first-named Siṃhapura as the homeland of Vijaya is clear from the fact that even in later times two Indian princes, Nissaṅkamalla and Sāhasamalla, from the royal house of this place, were successively offered the throne of Ceylon.[2] But if Siṃhapura, the homeland of Vijaya, were situated in western Bengal or southern India, there is no reason why the ship which carried Vijaya and his councillors and officers touched the western coast of India at the ports of Bharukaccha (Broach) and Suppāraka (Sopārā) and proceeded therefrom to reach the western shore of Ceylon. It is equally unintelligible why another ship was carrying Vijaya's wife and her female companions to Mahilādīpa, which was undoubtedly an island governed by women and situated, according to Megasthenes[3] and Hiuen Tsang,[4] below Persia and near the mouth of the Indus. The identification of Lāḷa by Geiger with Lāṭa on the western coast of India above Gujarat does not wholly meet the situation. The oldest form of the Sinhalese language, as found in the early Brāhmī inscriptions, appears as an Indo-Aryan dialect, which is very closely allied to the language of the Mansehra version of Asoka's Rock Edicts. In accounting for all these facts the historian cannot but think of Siṃhapura in the lower eastern Punjab.

The change of the genitive suffix *sya* (Pali *ssa*) into *ha* is a distinctive characteristic of old Sinhalese, which is without

---

[1] Watters, *On Yuan Chwang*, II, p. 233.
[2] *Cūḷavaṃsa*, P.T.S., Chap. 80, vv. 18 foll.
[3] McCrindle, *Ancient India*, p. 150.
[4] Watters, *On Yuan Chwang*, II, p. 257.

its parallel in any of the earlier known inscriptions of India. This goes to connect the language with Old Persian in which we have *hyā* for *sya* and the Dardic speech of Dardistan.[1] It is near about Dardistan that there still dwell a people called Singhans, i.e. Siṃhalas (Pali Sīhaḷas).

The chronicles of Ceylon have nothing to say about the Uttarāpatha background of the ancient history of Ceylon. They will offer us cheap and fantastic explanations for the origin of the two names of the island, Sīhaḷa because of the epithet Sīhaḷa earned by Vijaya's father Sīhabāhu since he had slain the lion,[2] and Tambapaṇṇi because of the fact that on their first landing on the island the hands of Vijaya's companions were coloured red with the dust of the red earth. While playing on the word *tambapāṇi*, 'red hand', they betray their ignorance of the fact that Tambapaṇṇi was just a Pali equivalent of the Sanskrit name Tāmraparṇī or Tāmravarṇī, meaning the copper-coloured or red-coloured.

The matrimonial alliances between the royal house and nobles of Ceylon and those of the neighbouring country of Pāṇḍya are not unexpected. The island may have needed the services of the traditional eighteen guilds from Pāṇḍya for her town-planning and industrial development. The building of the towns of Tambapaṇṇi and Anurādhapura with its suburbs by Vijaya and the princes and councillors who accompanied him is apparently too realistic to be disbelieved, although the fact may be that the work was not accomplished all at once.

After setting up Vijaya as the king eponymous of Ceylon the chroniclers seem interested in building up a *rāja-paramparā* parallel to that of Magadha: from Vijaya to Devānaṃpiya Tissa, from Ajātasattu to Dhammāsoka. Thereafter the thread of synchronism is lost, and it can be rarely established in individual cases on the joint evidence of the chronicles of Ceylon and other independent records.

The year of the Buddha's demise as known nowadays in Ceylon, Siam and Burma is 543 B.C. But the Buddha Era of 483 B.C. was current in Ceylon up till the fifteenth century, at the close of which a reform of the calendar was made. 483 B.C. agrees very nearly with 486 B.C., which is fixed on the strength of the Chinese dotted record maintained at Canton till the end of the year A.D. 489 and 487 B.C., which may be fixed on the strength of the contemporaneity of Devānaṃpiya Asoka with the five Greek kings.[3] In accord-

---

[1] Barua, *Ceylon Lectures*, p. 45, f.n. 4. [2] *Mahāvaṃsa*, Chap. 7, v. 42.

[3] *J.R.A.S.*, 1905, p. 51; *ibid.*, 1906, pp. 984ff.; *Epi. Zeyl.*, III, pp. 4ff.; *J.R.A.S.*, Ceylon Branch, XXIII, No. 67, pp. 141ff.; Barua, *Asoka and His Inscriptions*, I, pp. 6ff.

ance with the Buddha Era of 483 B.C. Geiger presents the chronicle tables of the kings of Ceylon and Magadha as below:

		B.C.			B.C.
1.	Vijaya ..	.. 483–445	1.	Ajātasattu ..	491–459
	Interregnum	.. 445–444	2.	Udayabhadda ..	459–443
2.	Paṇḍu Vāsudeva	.. 444–414	3.	Anuruddha and Muṇḍa	443–435
			4.	Nāgadāsaka ..	435–411
3.	Abhaya ..	.. 414–394	5.	Susunāga ..	411–393
	Interregnum	.. 394–377	6.	Kālāsoka ..	393–365
4.	Paṇḍuka Abhaya	.. 377–307	7.	Ten sons of Kālāsoka	365–343
			8.	Nine Nanda brothers	343–321
			9.	Candagutta ..	321–297
5.	Muṭasiva	.. 307–247	10.	Bindusāra ..	297–269
6.	Devānampiya Tissa	247–207	11.	Dhammāsoka ..	269–232

The immediate successor of king Vijaya is said to have been Paṇḍuvāsa [1] or Paṇḍuvāsudeva [2] who was the youngest brother of Vijaya and reigned for thirty years. The change of the *Dīpavaṃsa* name Paṇḍuvāsa into Paṇḍuvāsudeva must have been purposely done in the later chronicle *Mahāvaṃsa*, the author of which seems to have been somehow acquainted with the name of Pauṇḍravāsudeva, king of Vaṅga and Kaliṅga, mentioned in the *Mahābhārata* in connection with the military campaign of Bhīma.[3] But the earlier name Paṇḍuvāsa meaning the pale-robed one would seem more appropriate in view of the account given in the *Mahāvaṃsa* of his arrival in Ceylon with a retinue of thirty-two followers, all in the guise of Indian wandering ascetics (*paribbājakaliṅgavā*). The later chronicle supersedes the earlier one in mentioning the mouth of the river Mahākandara [4] as the landing place of Paṇḍuvāsudeva and his retinue.[5] From this place they are said to walk down to Upatissagāma, a locality in a suburb of Anurādhapura.

Another happy coincidence is devised for a critical juncture when a suitable princess was needed to be the queen of Paṇḍuvāsa. The princess supplied is a Śākya maiden called Kaccānā or Bhaddakaccānā who arrived on the island precisely with a retinue of thirty-two maidens. The story of matrimonial alliance of the royal house with a Śākya royal house of a kingdom founded on the southern bank of the Ganges, was thought to be an attractive prelude to a course of events leading to the establishment of the Buddhist faith in the island. The foundation of a new Śākya territory on the southern bank of the Ganges needed a plausible explanation,

---

[1] *Dīpavaṃsa*, X, 2. [2] *Mahāvaṃsa*, VIII, 10.

[3] *Mbh.*, Sabhā P., Chap. 34, v. 11 (Vaṅgavāsī Edn.).

[4] *Mahāvaṃsa*, VIII, 12. According to Geiger, it was probably a small stream to the north of Mannar.

[5] *Ibid.*, VIII, 12.

and it was found in the historical tradition of the massacre of the Śākyas by Viḍūḍabha the usurper king of Kośala in the last year of the Buddha's life.[1] The same is utilized by the chroniclers of other places for explaining the foundation of Śākya territories elsewhere.[2] I have shown elsewhere that the story of the decimation of the Śākyas in the Buddha's life-time is falsified by the Pali canonical representation of the Śākyas of Kapilavatthu as one of the powerful claimants for the bodily remains of the Buddha.[3]

The earlier chronicle has nothing more to say than this that the Śākya princess Kaccānā who came to the island from Jambudīpa (India) became the chief queen of Paṇḍuvāsa. The relationship of Paṇḍuvāsa with Vijaya is not mentioned, nor is it said that he came across from India. The *Dīpavaṃsa* is silent about the territory from which Kaccānā came and the circumstances under which she had to leave her father's territory.[4] The missing links are ingeniously supplied in the *Mahāvaṃsa*. We are told that the princess Bhaddakaccānā, too, came in a ship with her retinue, all in the guise of female wandering ascetics (paribbājikā)[5] evidently to evade the risk of being attacked by pirates on the way. The fascination of the number thirty-three for the chronicler lay apparently in the theological motive to suggest that the island was converted into a heaven of the thirty-three gods and goddesses.

The chronicles did not stop there. They would bring into the island the seven Śākya princes, all grandsons of Amitodana, a brother of Suddhodana, to figure as seven gāmaṇīs or village headmen.[6] The seven settlements of these princes, all brothers of Bhaddakaccānā, were respectively named after them as Rāmagāma, Tissagāma, Anurādhagāma, Mahāligāma, Dīghāvugāma, Rohiṇīgāma.[7] The Mahāvaṃsa omits the name of Tissa and spells the name of the seventh prince as Rohaṇa. It credits Anurādha also with the excavation of a tank to the south of Anurādhagāma.[8]

The parallelism between the two *rāja-paramparās* is brought out thus in the *Dīpavaṃsa*: In the ninth year of Ajātasattu's reign Vijaya came to Ceylon. In the sixteenth year of Udaya's reign Paṇḍuvāsa was crowned. In the

---

1 *Mahāvaṃsa*, VIII, 18-19.

2 Watters, *On Yuan Chwang*, I, p. 238.

3 B. C. Law, *Some Kṣatriya Tribes of Ancient India*, Chap. V.

4 *Dīpavaṃsa*, X, 1-2.

5 *Mahāvaṃsa*, VIII, 24: The landing place of the princess is said to have been Goṇagāma apparently at the mouth of the same river called *Mahākandara*.

6 *Dīpavaṃsa*, X, 6-7; *Mahāvaṃsa*, IX, 15.

7 *Dīpavaṃsa*, Chap. X.

8 *Mahāvaṃsa*, Chap. IX, vv. 9–11.

interval between the two kings, Vijaya and Paṇḍuvāsa, the island had no king for one year. In the twenty-first year of Nāgadāsa Paṇḍuvāsa died and Abhaya was crowned. In the fourteenth year of Candagutta king Pakuṇḍaka died and his son Muṭasiva was consecrated. In the eighteenth year of Asoka king Muṭasiva died to be succeeded by his son Devānampiya Tissa.[1] Pakuṇḍaka of the *Dīpavaṃsa* is the same king as Paṇḍuka Abhaya of the *Mahāvaṃsa*, father of Muṭasiva and grandfather of Tissa. The identity of the two is suggested in the *Dīpavaṃsa* itself.[2]

The royal line of Vijaya, better of Paṇḍuvāsa, became deflected when the rulership of the island was seized by Pakuṇḍaka or Paṇḍuka Abhaya after slaying seven of his maternal uncles, the younger brothers of king Abhaya, who died after a successful reign of twenty years. On his paternal side Paṇḍuka Abhaya is represented as the grandson of the Śākya prince who figured in the island as Dīghāvu the clever Gāmaṇī.[3] It is interesting to note how the chroniclers availed themselves of the Indian legend of Devagabbhā, Nandagopā, Vāsudeva and Kamsa as contained in the Ghata Jātaka.[4]

It is certain that Devānampiya Tissa who was definitely a Ceylon contemporary of Devānampiya Asoka was preceded by a line of kings, even if we prefer with Dr. Paranavitana to regard them as elected leaders and not as properly consecrated rulers. The royal line which commenced from the reign of Pakuṇḍaka or Paṇḍuka would seem quite historical. The earlier framework of the political history of Ceylon is more or less a got up thing. The true significance of the *Dīpavaṃsa* name Paṇḍuvāsa is still a matter of speculation. I have taken it so far to mean the pale-robed one, but it may as well be a Pali or Prakrit equivalent of Pāṇḍyavarṣa meaning one from the Pāṇḍya country, i.e. a Pāṇḍya by his nationality. The name Paṇḍuka is apparently of the same import. According to Megasthenes the Pāṇḍyas were originally a people who maintained the tradition of a matriarchal form of society.[5]

Assuming that the political history of Ceylon began from the reign of Paṇḍuka, it is important to note how his career is described in the chronicles. He rose into power and eminence from the family of a village headman and popular leader.[6] He started his career as a robber with the forest as his hiding

---

[1] *Dīpavaṃsa*, XI, 8-14.

[2] *Ibid.*, X, 9; XI, 1-2.

[3] *Ibid.*, X, 8.

[4] *Jātaka*, No. 454.

[5] McCrindle, *Ancient India*, p. 150.

[6] Cf. Mehergrām Copperplate Inscription of Dāmodaradeva which records an Indian instance of the rise of the Deva dynasty of Samatata from the family

place. The first definite step to seizing the rulership was to get rid of his rivals. After obtaining the rulership his first duty was to establish peace and order in the country. The chronicles credit him with an unusual length of reign for seventy years. His son and successor Muṭasiva, too, is said to have reigned for sixty years. The earlier chronicle skips over a very important matter relating to Paṇḍuka's reign, which is dealt with in the *Mahāvaṃsa*. It appears that in building up Anurādhapura into a fine and prosperous city, evidently on the site of Anurādhagāma, he faithfully followed the Indian system of town-planning and town administration.

The city was provided with four gates, each of which opened into a *dvāragāma* or suburb. Four tanks were caused to be made, one on each side, all named after Abhaya. The city was guarded by the Yakkha shrines on the four sides, that of the Yakkha Kāḷavela on the east side, that of the Yakkha Cittarāja on the same side at the lower end of the Abhaya-tank, that of a Yakkhinī at the south gate, the Banyan shrine of the Yakkha Vessavana Kubera presumably at the north gate, and the Palmyra-palm shrine of Vyādhideva presumably at the west gate.[1] Within the precincts of the royal palace was built the central shrine of an Assamukhī yakkhiṇī. To all of these demi-gods and demi-goddesses the sacrificial offerings were caused to be made year by year, while on festival days the king sat beside the image of Cittarāja on a seat of equal height and having the dolls of gods and goddesses and human dancers to dance before them. Similarly the charity-halls were put up on the four sides.[2]

The city was caused to be guarded by a city-warden (*nagara-guttika*). On its western side were quartered the *caṇḍālas* who did the work of sweepers, cleaners of sewers, corpse-bearers and watchers of the cemetery. The *caṇḍālas* had a separate cemetery for their use to the north-east of their locality. North of the *caṇḍāla* cemetery and between it and the Pāsāṇa mountain were built the huts for the huntsmen (*vyādhas*). In the space to the north of these and extending as far as the *Gāmaṇī* tank was built a hermitage for the hermits (*tāpasas*). To the east of the same *caṇḍāla* cemetery was built a house for the Nigaṇṭha (Jaina recluse) Jotiya, and in that locality dwelt the Nigaṇṭha called Giri and the recluses (*samaṇas*) of various orders. A temple

---

1 *Mahāvaṃsa* (X, 89-90) wrongly places the shrines of Vessavana and Vyādhideva on the western side.

2 *Mahāvaṃsa* (X, 90) places them only on the western side. Geiger and others have failed to make out the right word *dānasaṃbhāgavatthuṃ*; here *yonasabhāgavatthuṃ* is meaningless.

(*devakula*) was caused to be built for the Nigaṇṭha Kumbhaṇḍa, which was named after him. Westward of these and eastward of the huts of huntsmen dwelt five hundred families of heretical faith. Beyond Jotiya's house and on this side of the *Gāmaṇī* tank were caused to be built a retreat for the wandering ascetics (*paribbājakārāma*), and an abode for the Ājīvikas, and a residence for the Brāhmaṇas.

Here the city of Anurādhapura as built by Paṇḍuka Abhaya appears as a Ceylon counterpart of an Indian city like Rājagaha, Vesālī or Pāṭaliputta. Whether all the details given in the *Mahāvaṃsa* about it, when it was first built, be literally true or not, the religious conditions and atmosphere which prevailed in the island previous to the reign of Devānampiya Tissa and the propagation of Buddhism are precisely the same as those presupposed by the 13th Rock Edict of Asoka. The hermits, Brahman wandering ascetics, Ājīvikas, Jaina and other recluses were the precursors of the Buddhist missionaries and preachers as much as in India as in Ceylon. They were the pre-Asokan and pre-Tissa evangelists of the Indo-Aryan culture who prepared the ground for Buddhism.[1] The island had the age-old shrines of the Yakkhas, Rākkhasas, Pisācas and Nāgas. Mahinda, the king of the gods, had been the guardian deity of Laṅkā before Mahinda, the propagator of Buddhism, took over the charge of the island. The ascetic god Śiva had a good deal of hold over the religious belief of the people, and it is manifest even from the personal names of Girikaṇḍasiva and king Muṭasiva, father of Tissa. The god Uppalavaṇṇa or Viṣṇu was the intermediary between the two Mahindas.

The contemporaneity of Tissa with Asoka, both honoured with the same epithet, is shown to have afforded an important junction for the meeting of the three lines of chronological succession, namely, the *rājaparamparās* of Magadha and Ceylon and the *theraparamparā* of the orthodox Buddhist order. Thus the chronicles enjoy a triple importance through their bearings on the early political histories of India and Ceylon and the early history of Buddhism. As regards Ceylon, the political, social and religious background of this junction has already been discussed and characterized. The three main landmarks of the early history of Buddhism from the demise of the Buddha are the three orthodox councils (*saṃgītis*), each preceded by a general gathering of the monks (*sannipāta*), out of which the delegates were selected. In

---

[1] Law, *India as described in early texts of Buddhism and Jainism*, pp. 218ff.; McCrindle, *Ancient India*, pp. 69, 106, 120.

connection with the councils the three royal patrons are said to have gained in importance, namely, Ajātasattu, Kālāsoka and Dhammāsoka. While judging the success of a reign three main considerations rest on the chroniclers' decision: (i) the removal of the undesirable elements and the quelling of the disturbing factors with a view to making the island a fit habitat for the higher races of men, (2) the works of piety and public utility, and (3) the aids to the cause of religion and religious foundations and the development of art and architecture. From the Buddhist point of view too, the main grounds of consideration are: (1) the patronage to the orthodox order in the task of collecting the traditional teachings of the Buddha, handing them down by an oral tradition or preserving them by means of writing, and promoting the cause of Buddhist education and scholarship, (2) the aids to the same in maintaining its activity and integrity by getting the help of the heretics and schismatics, and (3) the stabilization of the position of Buddhism and enhancement of its popularity through the erection of magnificent monasteries (*ārāmas*, *vihāras*) and Buddhist shrines, particularly the *thūpas* or dagobas, the latter as tangible means of keeping up the memory of the Buddha and other great personages among his disciples and followers. Judged by all the six considerations Devānampiya Asoka of India was sure to be found the best monarch on the earth who appeared to the chroniclers as a living embodiment of the *cakkavattī* ideal of the Buddha. It was then natural to them to idolize as much Dhammāsoka of Jambudīpa as their own Devānampiya Tissa.

To honour Devānampiya Tissa as the first great builder the *Mahāvaṃsa* preserves the following traditional list of memorable erections: the Mahāvihāra and Cetiyavihāra, the Thūpārāma and Mahāthūpa, the shrine of Mahābodhi, a stone-pillar before the Mahācetiya or Mahāthūpa bearing an inscription, the Collar-bone shrine at Mahiyaṅgaṇa, the Issarasamaṇaka Vihāra on the spot where Mahinda converted five hundred votaries of Issara meaning Śiva, the Tissa Tank, the Paṭhama Thūpa at the landing place of Mahinda, the Vessagiri Vihāra at the place where Mahinda converted five hundred men of the Vessa caste, the delightful Upāsikāvihāra, Hatthāḷhaka Vihāra and two nunneries, the Jambukoḷa Vihāra at the port of Jambukoḷa in Nāgadīpa, and the Tissa Mahāvihāra and Pācīnavihāra at Anurādhapura.[1]

The *rājaparamparā* of Magadha as presented in the chronicles shows the succession of four ruling dynasties: the

[1] *Mahāvaṃsa*, XX, 17–25.

dynasty traced from Bhātiya, father of Bimbisāra, and a friend and contemporary of Suddhodana, father of Gotama the Buddha, the Susunāga (Śaisunāga), the Nanda, the Moriya (Maurya). They were unaware of the fact that the rulers of the first dynasty were known as Haryaṅkas.[1] The Purāṇas treat the first two dynasties as one and apply to it the name of Śiśunāga or Śaiśunāga. The chronicles are not concerned with the Bṛhadrathas who were the precursors of the Haryaṅkas. It is on the whole found that the chronological succession of the rulers of Magadha from Bhātiya as suggested in the chronicles is the most reliable of all. The Buddhist Sarvāstivāda tradition is defective for a two-fold reason: (1) that it ignores the history of a century, and (2) that it is guilty of a confusion between Kālāsoka the Susunāga and Dhammāsoka the Moriyan. The importance of Ajātasattu is stressed on two grounds: (1) the collection of the bodily remains of the Buddha from all the *thūpas* in which they were at first enshrined for depositing them in one thūpa built at Rājagaha, and (2) the facilities offered to the five hundred leading Theras when they met at the First Council for the collection of the words of the Buddha and the preparation of the first redaction of the Theravāda or Pali Canon.

With regard to the first wise deed of Ajātasattu for facilitating the great work to be done by Dhammāsoka the chronicles sought to establish an island parallel in a similar deed on the part of Devānampiya Tissa with reference to the great work to be done by Duṭṭhagāmaṇi Abhaya who was the national hero of Ceylon in the estimation of Mahānāma, the famous author of the *Mahāvaṃsa.* Unexpectedly the account given of the Rājagaha Thūpa of Ajātasattu with all the details of its construction[2] is highly exaggerated. This account presupposes not only a Buddhist stūpa in India, such as that of Bhārhut completed as late as 100 B.C., but also even those built in Ceylon in the time of Duṭṭhagāmaṇi.

As regards the part played by Ajātasattu in connection with the First Buddhist Council, the Pali Canonical account in the Vinaya Cullavagga, Chap. XI, is completely silent. The chronicles while giving an account of the First Council overstep certain limits set in the earlier and more authentic Vinaya description. The latter, for instance, does not associate the place of the Council with the Sattapaṇṇi Cave, nor does it tell us that the three Piṭakas were brought into existence by the Theras under the leadership of Mahākassapa.

---

[1] B. C. Law, *Aśvaghoṣa*, p. 80.

[2] *Sumaṅgalavilāsinī*, ii, pp. 611ff.; *Thūpavaṃsa*, pp. 34-35.

The description goes only so far as to state that the nucleus of the Buddhist canon was formed by the five Nikāyas and two Vinaya books, namely, the *Bhikkhu-vibhaṅga* and the *Bhikkhunī-vibhaṅga*.[1]

It is true that the Vinaya account of the Second Buddhist Council, too, clearly points to 100 B.C. as an important chronological landmark of the early history of Buddhism, and the fact is corroborated by the internal evidence of a few other Canonical texts.[2] It may be true that 100 B.E. fell within the reign of Kālāsoka, identified by Dr. Raychaudhuri with Kākavarṇa of the Purāṇas. But the Vinaya description is reticent on the part played by Kālāsoka in the matter of the Council itself. There is another important point of difference to which the reader's attention must be drawn.

All that the Vinaya account offers us is a description of the general conference of the Theras which appointed a judicial committee of eight representatives to give its considered findings on the ten issues arising from the indulgences of the Vajjiputtaka monks of Vesālī in contravention of Vinaya rules.

It has nothing to say regarding the Second Council convened to recite and canonize the authoritative Buddhist texts and the Great Council (*Mahāsaṅgīti*) convened by the Vajjiputtaka monks for vindicating their position as against the arbitrary action of the orthodox Theras. It is reticent also on the rise of the eighteen Buddhist sects and schools of thought previous to the reign of Aśoka as a sequel to the first rupture brought about in the Saṅgha by the Vajjiputtaka seceders.

These three deficiencies are made good in the chronicles. That the Vinaya description is incomplete without the account of the Second Council proper may be taken for granted, otherwise the incorporation of some texts and compilations into the growing corpus of the Buddhist Canon, even such texts as the Vinaya *Mahāvagga* and *Cullavagga*, the *Serissakavatthu* and several discourses with reference to Pāṭaliputta, is inexplicable. It seems very likely that the high-handed action on the part of the orthodox section of the Buddhist brotherhood of the age was bound to be followed by a schismatic reaction. This eventuality is equally borne out by the Sarvāstivāda tradition as embodied in the writings of Vasumitra, Bhavya and Vinītadeva. The Chinese pilgrim

---

[1] *Vinaya Piṭaka*, edited by Oldenberg, II, p. 287.

[2] The Serissaka story forming the canon basis of the *Vimāna* and *Petavatthus* professes to be a composition of 100 B.E. B. C. Law, *History of Pali Literature*, Vol. I, p. 36.

Hiuen Tsang, too, was well aware of the tradition about the eighteen sects. Unfortunately even Vasumitra, the earliest among the Sarvāstivāda writers, cannot be supposed to have flourished in an age anterior to the reign of the Kuṣāṇa king Kaṇiṣka. The reliability of the Ceylon tradition about the rise of the eighteen sects prior to Asoka's time is doubted for the first time by Dr. D. R. Bhandarkar on the strength of the evidence of the three versions of Asoka's Schism Pillar Edicts at Sārnāth, Kauśāmbī and Sāñcī [1] and subsequently discussed at length by Dr. Barua,[2] and in the opinion of both the history of the rise of these earlier Buddhist sects must have to be relegated to a post-Asokan period. The utmost concession which could be made to the Ceylon tradition is that the unorthodox views discussed in the *Kathāvatthu* which is traditionally a compilation of the eighteenth year of Asóka's reign, were the views of individual members and their adherents within one and the same *Saṅgha* and not those of separate sects and schools of thought whose names figure prominently in Indian inscriptions, none of which can be dated earlier than the first century B.C. and later than the third century after Christ. Buddhaghosa, the author of the *Kathāvatthu Commentary*, clearly distinguishes between the views as upheld by the individual teachers and their supporters in Asoka's time, and the same as upheld in his days by the different Buddhist sects and schools. The author of the *Nikāya-saṅgraha* suggests an ingenious way out of the difficulty by stating that the Tīrthakas who had been expelled from the Saṅgha in Asoka's time on account of their non-conformity with the rules of the Canon grew angry and assembled at Nālandā. They deliberated together with a view to causing a breach among the Śākya monks. Determined to become monks again, they returned, and failing to gain admission into the Theriya order, they went to the fraternities of the seventeen schismatic sects, the Mahāsaṅghika and the rest. Even these orders they left afterwards, and after two hundred and thirty-five years from the Buddha's demise they separated into six divisions and resided in six places giving rise to nine later sects: Hemavata, Rājagiri, Siddhārtha, Pūrvaśailī, Aparaśailī, Vājirī, Vaitulya, Andhaka and Anya-mahāsaṅghika.[3]

Thus the author of a Sinhalese chronicle of the fourteenth century tried to reconcile the earlier available Ceylon tradi-

[1] *Asoka*, revised Ed., p. 100.

[2] Barua, *Asoka and His Inscriptions*, Pt. I, pp. 333ff.

tions regarding the rise of the Buddhist schismatics as several sects both before and after Asoka. They are apparently guilty of an anachronism. The Schism Pillar Edict of Asoka promulgates an ordinance, meaning to penalize those who will cause a division in the *Saṅgha* (*ye bhākhati*, future tense), while the Ceylon traditions tell us that Asoka actually penalized the schismatics. Here is a glaring instance of confusion between the future on the one hand and present and past on the other.

The *Dīpavaṃsa* says nothing about the Nandas. Incidentally it refers to the reign of Candagutta of the Moriya family (*Moriya-kula*).[1] The gap between the Susunāgas and the Moriyas is filled up by the Mahāvaṃsa [2] with the reign of the Nine Nandas. In the latter work Candagutta is said to have killed Dhanananda, the last Nanda king, and secured the sovereignty over the whole of Jambudīpa under the guidance of the wrathful Brāhman Cāṇakka (Cāṇakya). The *Mahāvaṃsa-Ṭīkā* goes still further to avail itself of a fantastic story to account for the name of Candagutta and of other legends to connect Candagutta and his descendants with the Moriyas, undoubtedly the Moriyas of Pipphalivana, and ultimately with the Śākyas of Kapilavatthu. It narrates the early life and training of Candagutta under Cāṇakka.[3] Evidently there grew up in later times a Ceylon Buddhist version of the legend of Candagutta and Cāṇakka as a counterpart of the Brahmanical and Jaina versions.

With the chroniclers of Ceylon Bindusāra, the son and successor of Candagutta, is just a passing shadow. They are unaware of the legend of Bindusāra in the *Mañjuśrī Mūlakalpa*.

The historical value of the Pali legendary materials for the life and career of Asoka has been carefully discussed and assessed by competent scholars.[4] But it may not be out of place to state below some of the main results hitherto obtained. It is opined that these legends are not altogether fictitious. They are of great value only in so far as they supplement the information which can be gathered from the inscriptions and Greek writings. They are certainly one-sided and inconclusive. There was distinctly a Buddhist theological motive behind the connection which is sought to be established between the Moriyas of Magadha with the Moriya clan of warriors and ultimately with the Śākyas. In many respects

---

1 *Dīpavaṃsa*, VI, 19. 2 *Mahāvaṃsa*, V, 66.

3 *Vaṃsatthappakāsinī*, I, pp. 183ff.

4 Rhys Davids, *Buddhist India*, pp. 274ff.; Radhakumud Mookerji, *Asoka*, 9; Barua, *Asoka and His Inscriptions*, Pt. I, pp. 7ff.

the legends are irreconcilable with Asoka's own records. On the whole the tradition preserved in the *Dīpavaṃsa* is most helpful to the modern historian, particularly with regard to the double conversion and coronation of Asoka.

The main concern of the Ceylon chroniclers about Asoka is to represent him as the greatest known Buddhist emperor of Jambudīpa, as the greatest builder of Buddhist *vihāras* and religious monuments, and as the greatest supporter of the Buddhist faith and missionary activities. The vital point in which the inscriptions are apt to disappoint them is the lack of corroboration of the truth in the legend claiming Mahinda and Saṅghamittā to be beloved children of Asoka by his Vaiśya wife Devī of Vidisā. Until the thirteenth or fourteenth year of Asoka his children were completely out of the picture (R.E. V). None can think of Asoka having grown up sons before his 27th regnal year (P.E. VII). Some amount of suspicion is sure to arise in connection with the chronicle story of Mahinda's coming to the island through the air, and this is enhanced by the more probable story narrated by Hiuen Tsang that Mahinda's missionary work had been directed to the country of Malayakūṭa which is no other than Tāmraparṇī of the Great Epic, situated in the extreme south of the Deccan, below Pāṇḍya or Drāviḍa and Tambapaṇṇi of Asokan edicts (R.E. II and XIII). It is from the country of Malayakūṭa that Mahinda went across to Ceylon, the island of Tambapaṇṇi.

The Pali traditional account of the rise of the eighteen Buddhist sects or schools of thought during the century which elapsed between the reigns of Kālāsoka and Asoka and that of the heterodox views upheld by others, the Brāhmans, the Paṇḍaraṅga Parivrājakas, Ājīvikas, and Nirgranthas, who, led by the greed of gain, assumed the garb of monks and stealthily entered the Asokārāma at Pāṭaliputta, are irreconcilable. It is said that on account of the heresies advocated by them the orthodox monks declined to hold the *uposatha* or perform other ecclesiastical functions with them for a period of nine years. Asoka deputed a high official to request them to resume the *uposatha* and other duties, and when they declined to do so, he misunderstanding the intention of the king's order, beheaded some of them, an action deeply regretted by the king. To make amends for the blunder committed by his officer, Asoka caused a conference of the monks to be held at Pāṭaliputta for examining the inmates of the local monastery who were maintaining those views. They were examined by the leading Thera called Moggaliputta

presence, and those whose views did not tally with the Vibhajjavāda, known as the genuine doctrine of the Buddha, were disrobed and expelled. Thus the undesirable elements were got rid of. Thereafter the Theras who were the true followers of the Buddha could be persuaded to resume and carry on the *uposatha* and other ecclesiastical duties as usual. They convened a council, the third orthodox Buddhist Council at Pāṭaliputta under the presidency of Moggaliputta Tissa. The compilation and canonization of the *Kathāvatthu*, embodying accounts of the controversies which took place at the preceding conference and their results, formed the outstanding work of this Council, besides the usual rehearsal of the texts of the *Buddhavacana* as then known to the Buddhist community. The Council was followed by the despatch of Buddhist missions to different countries, situated mostly, if not all, within India. The missions were despatched on the initiative of Moggaliputta Tissa.

In the *Kathāvatthu* itself the points at issue are not referred to any person or sect. Each of them is discussed on its merit. Buddhaghosa, too, does not suggest that the points discussed arose from the views of any or all of the pre-Asokan eighteen sects. The sects which existed in his time are brought in only as distinct schools of thought who maintained the views that were advocated in Asoka's time by the outsiders who entered the Asokārāma in the garb of Buddhist monks. The eighteen sects and their later offshoots came to figure prominently in the Indian inscriptions which cannot be dated earlier than the first century B.C. and later than the beginning of the fourth century A.D. The author of the *Nikāyasaṅgraha* saw the difficulty and as a way out of it he came to suggest that the outsiders gained admission into the seventeen unorthodox sects after they had failed to enter the Orthodox order of the Theras. This does not solve the problem regarding the rise of the eighteen sects in pre-Asokan times. The chronology suggested in the Pali tradition of Ceylon is not identical with that offered by Vasumitra in his account of the sects.[1] The light which may be obtained from the Schism Pillar Edict of Asoka is that there arose in his time certain causes threatening the unity and integrity of the *Saṅgha*, but these were not of a formidable nature. The king was in a position to state that those causes could be easily removed and the *Saṅgha* could be rendered 'whole and entire' for all times to come.

[1] *Journal of the Department of Letters*, Calcutta University, Vol. I, Masuda, *Early Indian Buddhist Schools*.

The tradition concerning the despatch of Buddhist missions to different places in India and to two places outside India deserves more than a passing notice. Unfortunately a similar tradition is not traced in the works of other sects. Hiuen Tsang knew certainly of a tradition that the Thera Mahinda, a brother of Asoka, did his missionary work in the country of Malayakūṭa below Drāviḍa before he went across to the island of Siṃhala. Although the missionaries were sent on the authority of Moggaliputta Tissa, it is found that the places within India to which they are said to have gone are places where Asoka set up his edicts and inscriptions:

1. Kasmīra-Gandhāra	Asoka's Rock Edicts at Mansehra.
2. Yona ..	Rock Edicts at Shahbazgarhi in the district of Peshawar.
3. Mahiṣamaṇḍala ..	Rock and Minor Rock Edicts at Yerraguḍi in the Karnool district.
4. Mahāraṭṭha ..	Minor Rock Edict at Gavimaṭh and Pālkiguṇḍa.
5. Vanavāsa ..	Minor Rock Edict at Isila.
6. Aparānta ..	Rock Edicts at Sopārā.
7. Himavanta ..	Rock Edicts at Kālsi in the district of Dehra Dun.

The two places or countries which lay according to the chronicles outside India are Suvaṇṇabhūmi and the island of Laṅkā or Tambapaṇṇi. It is shown that the country of Tambapaṇṇi which finds mention in Asoka's Rock Edicts II and XIII is not necessarily the island of Tambapaṇṇi. It is apparently the country of Tāmraparṇī, modern Tinnevelly district, placed by the *Mahābhārata*, south of Pāṇḍya or Drāviḍa with Mt. Vaidūryaka as its rocky landmark, in that case it is no other than Hiuen Tsang's country of Malayakūṭa. There existed a land route, even till the time of Hiuen Tsang, connecting Aparānta and Karṇāṭa with the lower Kāverī Valley. It is therefore possible that a traveller starting from Vidisā and Ujjayinī could reach the country of Tambapaṇṇi below Pāṇḍya by following this land route along the banks of the Kāverī via Mahiṣamaṇḍala or Mysore. The journey further down to the island of Tambapaṇṇi was a matter of crossing the ferry.

As regards Suvaṇṇabhūmi, it is suggested that probably the original place-name was Suvaṇṇagiri, which was the seat of southern viceroyalty in Asoka's time in view of the fact that the *Dīpavaṃsa* description differs materially from that in the *Mahāvaṃsa.*[1]

The chronicles speak of two coronations of Devānampiya Tissa, the second taking place six months after the first, in honour of the presents from Asoka, his distinguished Indian friend and ally. According to Dr. Paranavitana the second coronation of Tissa was the proper form of royal coronation and the so-called coronations prior to that were simple ceremonies of electing popular leaders.

The *Dīpavaṃsa* alone speaks of two consecrations of Prince Piyadassana, the first under the title of Asoka, four years after his accession to the throne of Bindusāra, and the second under the title of Piyadassi, six years after the first.[2] Here the *Dīpavaṃsa* tradition representing 'Asoka' as a royal title assumed by Asoka must be preferred to the *Divyāvadāna* legend representing the same as a personal name given him by his father at the instance of his mother. The truth in the *Dīpavaṃsa* tradition is borne out by the evidence of the inscriptions of Asoka.[3]

The tradition of the fratricidal war through which Prince Piyadassana's way to his father's throne lay is not clearly supported by the evidence of Asoka's R.E. V. The *Divyāvadāna* speaks of the killing of one stepbrother, which is a more probable story, while the Ceylon chronicles tell us that Asoka killed all his ninety-nine half-brothers. The story of Tissarakkhā in the *Mahāvaṃsa* blackening the history of the closing period of Asoka's reign was derived evidently from a later Indian source and it reads in some respects like the story of Tisyarakṣitā in the *Divyāvadāna*. The *Divyāvadāna* story of the Ājīvika *guru* of Asoka's mother, predicting her son's accession to the throne of Magadha, could not have its counterpart in any Pali work of Ceylon earlier than the *Mahāvaṃsa-Ṭīkā*. The *Dīpavaṃsa* agrees with the *Divyāvadāna* in giving

[1] *Dīpav.*, VIII, 11:

Suvaṇṇabhūmiṃ gantvāna Soṇuttarā mahiddhikā |
niddhametvā pisācagaṇe mocesi bandhanā bahu ||

Mahāv., XII, 44-45:

Saddhiṃ Uttaratherena Soṇatthero mahiddhiko |
Suvaṇṇabhūmiṃ agamā, tasmiṃ tu samaye pana ||
jāte jāte rājagehe dārake ruddarakkhasī |
samuddato nikkhamitvā bhakkhayitvāna gacchati ||

Cf. *Samantapāsādikā*, I, pp. 68ff., where both the descriptions are given without any comment. The earlier chronicle does not place the country on the sea-shore and associates it with the Pisācas.

[2] *Dīpav.*, VI, 22–24.

[3] Barua, *Asoka and His Inscriptions*, Pt. I, pp. 16ff.

the credit for the conversion of Asoka to the Buddhist faith to an Elder, whether the Thera Nigrodha or Sthavira Samudra, and not to a novice of seven years of age, who is represented in the later chronicle as the posthumous son of Sumana, the elder stepbrother of Asoka. The interest of the *Dīpavaṃsa* lies also in the fact that it settles once for all the interpretation of Asoka's statement—*saṃghe upayite,* which occurs in his Minor Rock Edict.

Though the mystery of the personal relationship of Mahinda and Saṅghamittā with Asoka cannot be solved in the light of Asoka's own records, there is no valid reason as yet to dispute the fact of their going down to Ceylon for the propagation of Buddhism during the reign of king Devānaṃpiya Tissa. The real foundation of the history of Buddhism in Ceylon may be taken to have been laid through the establishment of the order of monks by Mahinda and that of the order of nuns by Saṅghamittā. The traditional succession of the Vinaya teachers is expressly traced from Mahinda in the *Vinaya Parivārapāṭha* compiled in Ceylon by a Thera named Dīpa, and the chronicle account of the Buddhist missions despatched to different countries is corroborated, partly at least, as shown by Geiger, by the relic-casket inscriptions in the Stūpas of Sāñchī and Sonāri, one of which preserves for us also the name of Moggaliputta. The chronicle account of the planting of a Bo-graft in the heart of Ceylon and that of the enshrinement of certain relics of the Buddha in some dagobas built in the time of Devānampiya Tissa may also be taken to be true.

As shown before the seventeenth chapter of the *Dīpavaṃsa* commences a new chronicle with these words:

'*Battiṃsa-yojanaṃ dīghaṃ aṭṭhārasahi vitthataṃ* ।
Yojanasata-āvaṭṭaṃ sāgarena parikkhitaṃ ॥
Laṅkādīpavaraṃ nāma sabbattha ratanākaraṃ ।
Upetaṃ nadītaḷākehi pabbatehi vanehi ca ॥
dīpaṃ purañ ca rājā ca upaddutañ ca dhātuyo ।
thūpaṃ dīpañ ca pabbataṃ uyyānaṃ bodhi bhikkhunī ॥
bhikkhu ca buddhaseṭṭho ca terasa honti te tahiṃ ।
ekadese caturonāmaṃ suṇātha mama bhāsato ॥'

'Thirty-two leagues in length, eighteen leagues in breadth, hundred leagues in circumference, surrounded by the ocean is the excellent island called Laṅkā, which is everywhere a mine of treasure. It possesses rivers and tanks, hills and forests. The island, the capital, the king, the trouble, the relics, the stūpa, the lake, the mountain, the garden, the Bo-tree, the bhikkhuṇī, the bhikkhu and the most exalted Buddha—

these are the thirteen themes. Listen when I speak of them, each in four names (in relation to four Ages).'

The *Dīpavaṃsa* presents here only a bare outline of the political history of Ceylon from Muṭasiva to Mahāsena. As for the religious history, the whole of Chap. XVII is devoted to the career of Mahinda which extended over two reigns, namely, that of Devānampiya Tissa and that of Uttiya, his brother and successor. The Theras of Ceylon were naturally interested in having before them a chronological succession of the leading Vinaya teachers from Mahinda onwards and a similar succession of the leading nuns from the time of Saṅghamittā. Though the first is missed in the chronicles themselves, it is preserved in the *Vinaya Parivāra*. The second is presented in Chap. XVIII of the earlier chronicle. Here the earlier chronicle credits Devānampiya Tissa with the erection of the Tissārāma, an excellent monastery named after him and the planting of a Bodhi graft at Mahāmeghavana.

For a systematic traditional history of Ceylon from Mahāsiva, the younger brother and successor of Uttiya, to Mahāsena, we cannot but depend on the *Mahāvaṃsa*. The *Ṭīkā* has hardly anything new to add to the information supplied in the text. The central figure of this part of the chronicle is king Duṭṭhagāmaṇi, the national hero of Ceylon and great builder of Buddhist religious monuments. The chronology of the kings as found in this and the earlier chronicle is now considered workable and generally correct.[1] Here the historical position of the chronicles may be partially tested by the evidence of the ancient inscriptions which are written in Asokan and later Brāhmī. Unfortunately, however, none of the names by which the early kings of Ceylon are introduced in these inscriptions is identical with that which occurs in the chronicles. The identifications so far suggested are just tentative.[2]

These inscriptions envisage a political history of Ceylon from Uttiya, the brother and successor of Devānampiya Tissa, to Gajabāhuka Gāmaṇi (A.D. 173–195), more definitely from Saddhā Tissa, the younger brother and successor of Duṭṭhagāmaṇi Abhaya, to Gajabāhuka Gāmaṇi.[3] The two main heroes, Devānampiya Tissa and Duṭṭhagāmaṇi, are still missed in them. The employment of *Devanapiya* as a royal honorific goes certainly to prove that the tradition of Asoka was maintained in Ceylon up till the second century A.D., if

---

[1] Wickremasinghe, On Riṭigala Inscriptions, *Epigraphia Zeyl.*, Vol. I, p. 143.
[2] *Ibid.*, Vol. I, pp. 141ff.
[3] *Ibid.*, Vol. I, pp. 141ff.

not still later. Although their language, the Elu, bears all the distinctive characteristics of a dialect once current in the lower Punjab, on the eastern side of the Indus and near about Mansehra, their Brāhmī letter-forms go to connect them first with Asoka's inscriptions at Isila (Northern Mysore) and subsequently with the Buddhist cave inscriptions of Western India. It will be highly important and interesting to see if they can be connected as well with the old Brāhmī inscriptions of Amarāvatī, Jagayyapeta and Nāgārjunikoṇḍa, particularly those at the last mentioned place.

So far as the ancient inscriptions of Ceylon go, they point to a much simpler state of things than what appears in the chronicles. It is difficult to think that anything of architectural importance and beauty was or could be built in the time of Devānampiya Tissa. The vigorous creative activity of the art and architecture of Ceylon began during the reign of Duṭṭhagāmaṇi and was continued through subsequent reigns. The *Dīpavaṃsa* accounts are scrapy and in some places clumsy and vague. The *Mahāvaṃsa* has clarified them in many respects. And yet it seems that the later chronicle has antedated some of the achievements.

According to both the chronicles, Duṭṭhagāmaṇi attained the paramount position in the early history of Ceylon by giving a crushing defeat to the Tamil hordes led by Eḷāra who appeared in the island as a horse-dealer. A graphic description of the battles fought and won is given in the *Mahāvaṃsa*. The coming of the merchants and traders from India is a fact, which is borne out by some of the ancient inscriptions of Ceylon. But no inscription is found until now to confirm the truth of the battles fought by Duṭṭhagāmaṇi with Eḷāra and his lieutenants.

The *Dīpavaṃsa* represents Duṭṭhagāmaṇi as the builder of a magnificent palace of nine storeys in height, while Mahā Tissa or Saddhā Tissa, his brother and successor, is given the credit for the erection of the Lohapāsāda or 'Brazen Palace'. Both of them figure equally as the builders of the Mahāthūpa. In the earlier description and estimation Duṭṭhagāmaṇi's fame was worthily emulated by Saddhā Tissa. In the later chronicle Duṭṭhagāmaṇi alone is highly extolled as the builder of the Lohapāsāda, the Mahāthūpa, and the Maricavaṭṭivihāra. The fame of Saddhā Tissa fades away before the heightened glory of the achievements of his elder brother. The *Dīpavaṃsa* names fourteen Theras who came down from India when the foundation of the Mahāthūpa was laid by Duṭṭhagāmaṇi without mentioning the centres of the Theravāda

Buddhism represented by them.[1] The list of places is supplied by the *Mahāvaṃsa*, and it is to all intents and purposes the same as that contained in one of the Nāgārjunikoṇḍa inscriptions.

The disturbed reign of Vaṭṭagāmaṇi, the son and successor of Saddhā Tissa, rightly engages the attention of the chroniclers. He figures prominently also in some of the ancient inscriptions of Ceylon. His fame rests on these three facts: (1) as the vanquisher of the Tamil usurpers, (2) as the king who caused the Pali Canonical texts to be committed to writing, and (3) as the builder of the Abhayagiri monastery. His seven lieutenants heartily co-operated with him in building up a memorable tradition of art and architecture standing as a lasting symbol of piety.

From Vaṭṭagāmaṇi's son down to Mahāsena one notices a smooth course of political history. The chief event to be noted in the religious history of the period is the rivalry between the Fraternity of the Mahāvihāra and the Abhayagiri Vihāra which led ultimately to the rise of a few Buddhist sects in Ceylon.

The earlier chronicle is unaware of the six later Buddhist sects that arose in India, and of the two sects, *the Dhammaruci* and *the Sāgaliya*, that arose in the island. Buddhaghosa, the author of the *Kathāvatthu-aṭṭhakathā*, was acquainted with the names and doctrines of the later Buddhist sects but with none of the sects in Ceylon.

Buddhaghosa, the author of the *Samantapāsādikā*, speaks of a serious dispute which arose in the Buddhist community of Ceylon over the legality of certain Vinaya rules. King Bhātika (Bhātu Tissa) heard the two parties in an assembly of the monks called for the purpose and decided the point at issue by the verdict given by his Brāhman minister named Dīghakārāyana.[2] The chronicles refer this incident to the reign of Abhaya or Vohārika Tissa, the son and successor of Sirināga. According to the earlier chronicle, the monks against whom Kapila, the minister of Tissa, expressed his judgment are described as 'wicked' (*pāpabhikkhu*),[3] while the later chronicle calls them upholders of *Vetullavāda* or *Vedallavāda*.[4] The *Dīpavaṃsa* term is definitely *Vitaṇḍavāda*.[5]

The *Mahāvaṃsa* tells us that the rival Abhayagiri Vihāra became a stronghold of the sixty monks preaching the Vetulya heresy, all of whom were banished from the island by

[1] *Dīpavaṃsa*, XIX, vv. 5–10.
[2] Cf. *Samantapāsādikā*, III, pp. 582-3.
[3] *Dīpavaṃsa*, XXII, 44.
[4] *Mahāvaṃsa*, XXXVI, 41.
[5] *Dīpavaṃsa*, XXII, 43.

Goṭhābhaya Meghavaṇṇa, the reigning king. We are also told that to avenge their cause a powerful Colian monk named Saṅghamitta, well versed in sorcery, witchcraft, and the like (*bhūtavijjādi-kovido*) came across from the Indian shore. It is said that he defeated the Mahāvihāra defender of the Theravāda by his arguments in an assembly of the monks caused to be called for the purpose by the king at Thūpārāma. The Thera Saṅghapāla was evidently then the head of the Mahāvihāra.[1] The crusade against the Mahāvihāra was vigorously led by this Saṅghamitta during the reign of Mahāsena, having Soṇa among the royal councillors as his strong lay supporter.[2] The *Dīpavaṃsa* makes mention of this mischievous activity and refers it in the same way to the reign of Mahāsena. But the heresies mentioned were not of a serious character, and they tended just to relax two Vinaya rules.[3]

Buddhaghosa in his commentary on the *Kathāvatthu*, has ascribed certain special views to the upholders of the *Vetullavāda*. The bearing of the *Mahāvaṃsa* report of the debate held at Thūpārāma between Saṅghamitta and the spokesman of the Mahāvihāra in the presence of king Goṭhābhaya Meghavaṇṇa, father of Mahāsena, and grandfather of Kitti-Siri-Meghavaṇṇa, on the contemporaneity and age of Buddhadatta and Buddhaghosa, the author of the Visuddhimagga, has been fully discussed. The authoritative works of the Vetullavādins mentioned in the *Sāratthappakāsinī* and the *Samantapāsādikā* have also been identified. They belonged mostly to the Guhyasamāja sect and the popular form of Mahāyāna. But the more appropriate name of the dreaded doctrine was rather *Vedallavāda* than *Vetullavāda*.[4]

The *Mahāvaṃsa* does nowhere clarify the connection of the two Buddhist sects of Ceylon, namely, *the Dhammaruci* and *the Sāgaliya*, with the Abhayagiri Vihāra and its seceders. The connection is supplied somewhat ingeniously in the *Ṭīkā* and the *Nikāyasaṅgraha*. These later works trace the history of the schisms in the Saṅgha of Ceylon from the days of Vaṭṭagāmaṇi. The author of the *Dīpavaṃsa* supplement (Chaps. XVII–XXII) had nothing to say regarding the cause which arose for the separation of the monks of Abhayagiri from the Mahāvihāra and the formation of the Dhammaruci sect under the persuasion of an Indian teacher, Dhammaruci, of the Vajjiputtaka community of Pallarārāma in South India.

---

1 *Mahāvaṃsa*, XXXVI, 110–116.
2 *Ibid.*, XXXVII, 28-29.
3 *Dīpavaṃsa*, XXII, 67–74.
4 *The University of Ceylon Review*, Vol. II.

It was during the reign of Vohāra Tissa that the Dhammarucikas of Abhayagiri adopted the *Vetulla* or *Vedalla Piṭaka*. The king caused the Vetulla books to be examined by his learned minister, Kapila, and finding that they were not the words of the Buddha, caused them to be burnt and the sinful priests to be disgraced. But from the account given by Buddhaghosa it appears that the difference hinged on a Vinaya point of minor importance. It was apparently a case of controversial nicety (*vitaṇḍavāda*) as the *Dīpavaṃsa* puts it.[1]

The ingenuity is evidently carried too far by the compiler of the *Nikāyasaṅgraha* when it wants us to believe that the Vetulla or Vedalla texts mentioned in the Pali commentaries were the works produced by the six later Buddhist sects of India, which arose in later times:

'The Hemavata heretics fabricated the *Warṇa-piṭaka*, giving it a semblance of true doctrine and making it appear as if preached by the Buddha. The Rājagiri heretics composed the *Aṅgulimāla-piṭaka*, the Siddhārthaka heretics the *Gūḍha Vessantara*, the Pūrvaśailī heretics the *Raṭṭhapāla-garjita*, the Aparaśailī heretics, the *Āḷavaka-garjita*, and the Wajraparvata heretics the *Gūḍhavinaya*. These last also composed the Tantras: *Māyājālatantra*,[2] *Samājatantra*, *Mahāsamayatattva*, *Tattvasaṅgraha*, *Bhūtacāmara* (*ḍāmara*),[3] *Vajrāmṛta*,[4] *Cakrasaṃvara*,[5] *Dvādaśacakra*, *Bherukādbuda*[6] *Mahāmāyā*,[7] *Padanikṣepa*, *Catuṣpuṣṭa*,[8] *Parāmarda*,[9] *Maricudbhava*, *Sarvabuddhasarvaguhyasamuccaya*,[10] etc., and the *Kalpa*-

---

[1] *Dīpavaṃsa*, XXII, vv. 43–45; *Mahāvaṃsa*, XXXVI, v. 41.

[2] *Māyājālatantra*. Cf. Commentary, *Māyājālamahātantra rājaṭikā*, *Rgyud*, LVI, 2; *Pañjikā*, *Rgyud*, LVI, 3. Probably the same as *Māyājālamahātantra*, Nanjio No. 1022, translated by Fa-Hien, A.D. 982–1001.

[3] *Bhūtaḍāmara tantra*—probably the same as *Bhūtaḍāmaramahātantrarāja*, Nanjio, No. 1031, translated by Fa-Hien in A.D. 973–981. Cf. *Bhūtaḍāmara-sādhana* and *Bhūtaḍāmara-saṅkhipta-sādhana*, P. Cordier, *Catalogue Du Fonds, Tibetan*, *Rgyud*, LXX, 164; LXXI, 337 and LXXXIII, 40.

[4] *Vajrāmṛta*. Nanjio (Nos. 372-373) mentions *Vajramantra-Dhāraṇī*.

[5] *Cakrasaṃvara* Cf. Commentary, *Cakrasaṃvara tantrarājasaṃvarasamuccaya*, Cordier, *op. cit.*, *Rgyud*, VIII, 1.

[6] *Bherukādbutatantra*. Cf. Commentary *Heruka-abhyudaya mahāyoginitantrarāja*, Cordier, *op. cit.*, *Rgyud*, XII, 2.

[7] *Mahāmayā*. Cf. Cordier, *op. cit.*, *Rgyud*, XXIII, 18. Cf. *Mahāmāyā sūtra*, Nanjio 382, translated in A.D. 550–577.

[8] *Catuṣpuṣṭa*. Cf. Commentary, *Catuḥpīṭha Gūḍhārthanirdeśa ekadruma-pañjikā*, Cordier, *op. cit.*, *Rgyud*, XXIII, 7.

[9] *Parāmara*. Cf. *Paramādi-tantrabhāṣitā pañcadaśāpatti*, Cordier, *op. cit.*, *Rgyud*, LXXXV, 55. Cf. *Paramārthadharmavijaya sūtra* and *Paramārtha-saṃvritinirdeśa sūtra*, Nanjio, Nos. 210-211, 1084, 1089 and 1101.

[10] *Sarvabuddha-Sarvaguhya samuccaya*. Cf. Commentaries *Sarvakalpa-samuccaya nāma Sarvabuddhasamayoga ḍākinījālasambarottarottara tantraṭikā*, Cordier, *op. cit.*, *Rgyud*, XXV, 2; *Pradīpa*, *Rgyud*, XLV, 24; *Sarvaguhya-pradīpaṭikā*, *Rgyud*, XXVIII, 3.

śāstras: Māyāmarīcikalpa, Herambakalpa, Trisamayakalpa,[1] *Rājakalpa, Wajragandhārakalpa,*[2] *Marīciguhyakalpa, Śuddha-samuccaya-kalpa,*[3] etc.

We are also told that the Vaitulya heretics composed the *Vaitulya Piṭaka*, the Andhakas, the *Ratnakūṭa Sūtra*[4] and other works, and the Anya-mahāsaṅghikas, the *Akṣarasāri*[5] and other sūtras.[6] The *Nikāyasaṅgraha* categorically states that despite many divisions that occurred, the religion of the Buddha retained its purity for two hundred and nineteen years from the Third Buddhist Council.[7]

The list of Buddhist works belonging to the *Vetulla* or *Vedalla Piṭaka* grew up gradually. According to the *Nikāya-saṅgraha*, the Vaitulya works were brought to Laṅkā on three successive occasions and burnt to ashes by sincere rulers. On the fourth occasion they were introduced by a merchant called Pūrṇa 852 years after the establishment of the Buddhist faith in the island during the reign of Devānaṃpiya Tissa and 1088 years after the demise of the Buddha.[8] On the first three occasions it was the Dharmarucikas of Abhayagiri who welcomed those texts which were incompatible with the true words of the Buddha. On the fourth occasion, however, the Dhammarucikas persuaded the Sāgaliyas of the Jetavana monastery to welcome them. It is said that during the reign of Aggabodhi I (A.D. 625–58) a Mahāthera named Jotipāla came down from India to try an issue with the Vaitulya heretics giving them a crushing defeat.[9] Thereafter there were no more converts to the Vetullavāda. It was again during the reign of Sena I (A.D. 887–907) that a Buddhist priest of the Vājiriya sect came to the island from India and dwelt in an abode called Vīraṅkura. He impressed the reigning king with his 'secret discourse', which he called a

[1] *Trisamayakalpa*. Cf. *Trisamayarājasādhana*, Cordier, *op. cit., Rgyud*, LXX, 5; LXXI, 95-96.

[2] *Wajragandhārakalpa*. Cf. *Vajragāndhārīsādhana*, Cordier, *op. cit., Rgyud*, LXX, 123; LXXI, 80.

[3] *Nikāyasaṅgraha*, p. 9.

[4] Nanjio No. 251—translated by An-shi-kao of the Eastern Han dynasty, A.D. 25–220. Nanjio No. 51, translated by Jnānagupta of the Sui dynasty A.D. 589–618.

[5] *Akṣarasāri Sūtra*, probably same as *Akṣaramatinirdeśa sūtra*, Nanjio No. 74. Translated by Dharmarakṣa of the Western Tsin dynasty A.D. 265–368. Nanjio No. 77—translated in the Earlier Sun dynasty A.D. 422–479.

[6] *Nikāya-saṅgraha*, pp. 9ff.

[7] *Ibid.*, p. 10.

[8] *Ibid.*, p. 17.

[9] *Cūḷavaṃsa*, 42, 35:

Tadā eko mahāthero Jotipālakanāmako
parājesi vivādena dīpe Vetullavādino. Cf. *Nikāya-saṅgraha*, p. 17.

confidential teaching. It was at this time that the *Ratnakūṭa* teaching and the like were introduced into Laṅkā.[1]

It will be seen that the Buddhist works mentioned above were all texts on ritual and magic. They were far from giving the Theras of Ceylon a correct idea of the greatness and excellence of Mahāyāna proper, the *Bodhisattva-naya* or *Agranaya form of Mahāyāna*. The doctrinal views ascribed by Buddhaghosa and Vasumitra to the *Pūrvaśailas*, the *Aparaśailas*, and the rest go only to represent them as advanced thinkers among the Buddhist teachers of the age.[2] The Theras of Ceylon were forgetful of the fact that their *Paritta texts* were also works on ritual and magic. The authenticity of the *Parittas* themselves was in dispute, and we have certain findings on this point from the Thera Nāgasena.[3]

As to the Mahāthera Jotipāla the chronicles leave us in the dark about his identity with the Bhadanta Jotipāla at whose instance Buddhaghosa undertook to write his commentaries on the *Saṃyutta and Aṅguttara Nikāyas*.[4] As a contemporary of king Aggabodhi I he was unquestionably a later personality.

According to the *Mahāvaṃsa-Ṭīkā* the Sāgalikas or Sāgaliyas were seceders from the Dhammarucikas. Their separation from the latter took place during the reign of king Goṭhābhaya and the name of the sect was derived from its leader, the Thera Sāgala.[5] The *Jetavana-vihāra* became the stronghold of this sect. The *Mahāvaṃsa-Ṭīkā* leads us to think that the Dhammarucikas and their offshoots, the Sāgalikas, possessed slightly different versions of the Vinaya texts.[6] The two sects belonging to the parent vihāra of Abhayagiri flourished side by side along with the Mahāvihāra, and continued to receive royal benefactions[7] until all of them were united into one order in the time of Parakkamabāhu I (A.D. 1153–86).[8]

[1] *Nikāya-saṅgraha*, p. 18.
[2] *Points of Controversy*, P.T.S. Tr., pp. xx ff.
[3] *Milinda*, pp. 150ff.
[4] B. C. Law, *Buddhaghosa*, p. 34.
[5] *Vaṃsatthappakāsinī*, p. 176.
[6] *Ibid.*, pp. 175-6, 676.
[7] *Cūḷavaṃsa*, XXXVIII, 75; XXXIX, 15, 41.
[8] *Ibid.*, LXXVIII, 21–27.

INDEX